Pneumatology: A Guide for the Perplexed

BLOOMSBURY GUIDES FOR THE PERPLEXED

Bloomsbury's Guides for the Perplexed are clear, concise and accessible introductions to thinkers, writers and subjects that students and readers can find especially challenging. Concentrating specifically on what it is that makes the subject difficult to grasp, these books explain and explore key themes and ideas, guiding the reader towards a thorough understanding of demanding material.

Guides for the Perplexed available from Bloomsbury include:

Atonement: A Guide for the Perplexed, Adam Johnson
Balthasar: A Guide for the Perplexed, Rodney Howsare
Benedict XVI: A Guide for the Perplexed, Tracey Rowland
Bonhoeffer: A Guide for the Perplexed, Joel Lawrence
Calvin: A Guide for the Perplexed, Paul Helm
De Lubac: A Guide for the Perplexed, David Grummett
Luther: A Guide for the Perplexed, David M. Whitford
Pannenberg: A Guide for the Perplexed, Timothy Bradshaw
Political Theology: A Guide for the Perplexed, Elizabeth Philips
Postliberal Theology: A Guide for the Perplexed,
Ronald T. Michener
Schleiermacher: A Guide for the Perplexed, Theodore Vial
Scripture: A Guide for the Perplexed, William Lamb
Tillich: A Guide for the Perplexed, Andrew O' Neil
Wesley: A Guide for the Perplexed, Jason A. Vickers
Žižek: A Guide for the Perplexed, Sean Sheehan

Forthcoming Guides for the Perplexed available from Bloomsbury include:

Barth: A Guide for the Perplexed, Paul T. Nimmo
Catholic Social Teaching: A Guide for the Perplexed,
Anna Rowlands
Ecumenism: A Guide for the Perplexed, R. David Nelson
God-Talk: A Guide for the Perplexed, Aaron B. James and
Ryan S. Peterson
Prayer: A Guide for the Perplexed, Ashley Cocksworth
Resurrection: A Guide for the Perplexed, Lidija Novakovic
Salvation: A Guide for the Perplexed, Ivor J. Davidson
Schillebeeckx: A Guide for the Perplexed, Stephan van Erp

Pneumatology

Daniel Castelo

A Guide for the Perplexed

Bloomsbury T&T Clark
An imprint of Bloomsbury Publishing Plc

B L O O M S B U R Y
LONDON • NEW DELHI • NEW YORK • SYDNEY

Bloomsbury T& T Clark

An imprint of Bloomsbury Publishing Plc

Imprint previously known as T&T Clark

50 Bedford Square	1385 Broadway
London	New York
WC1B 3DP	NY 10018
UK	USA

www.bloomsbury.com

BLOOMSBURY, T&T CLARK and the Diana logo are trademarks of Bloomsbury Publishing Plc

First published 2015

British Library Cataloguing-in-Publication Data
A catalogue record for this book is available from the British Library.

ISBN: HB: 978-0-567-46165-0
PB: 978-0-567-00680-6
ePDF: 978-0-567-65899-9
ePub: 978-0-567-65970-5

Library of Congress Cataloging-in-Publication Data
Castelo, Daniel, 1978–
Pneumatology : a guide for the perplexed / Daniel Castelo.
pages cm
ISBN 978-0-567-00680-6 (pbk) – ISBN 978-0-567-46165-0 (hbk) –
ISBN 978-0-567-65899-9 (epdf) – ISBN 978-0-567-65970-5 (epub)
1. Holy Spirit. I. Title.

BT121.3.C365   2015
231'.3–dc23

2014034178

Typeset by Newgen Knowledge Works (P) Ltd., Chennai, India

For Cheryl and Jackie

CONTENTS

ACKNOWLEDGMENTS

As for the immediate debts I have incurred during the process of writing this book, I wish to thank a number of colleagues for their recommendations and support. Although these shall remain anonymous, they were instrumental in making a case for my role as author of this work. I hope they are generally satisfied with the outcome. I also wish to thank the people of T & T Clark, particularly Anna Turton and Miriam Cantwell, for the invitation to write it and also for the patience needed to see it come to fruition. As I wrote the volume, I tested my work on an 8 a.m. class devoted to the doctrine of the Holy Spirit at Seattle Pacific University during the spring quarter of 2014; they provided a wonderful laboratory in which to present and probe the ideas herein; thanks, my dear students, for your help and earnestness. My "kindred spirit" in the academy, Robert Wall, gave me helpful feedback at various points of composition, for which I am grateful. Also, I would be remiss to not acknowledge the interrelation between pneumatology and music in my own life and work. In the case of this book, I should mention Frédéric Chopin, whose *Nocturnes* accompanied me at almost every step of composition; as I finished the text, I stumbled once more on J. S. Bach's *Mass in B Minor*, in particular the "Sanctus," which continues to provide me one of the most awe-inducing "glimpses of heaven" I have experienced in this life.

We are all learners before God and God's church. Therefore, I find it necessary to recognize my teachers for their role in shaping and forming me so as to help me be the kind of scholar who not only cares about pneumatology but has been impassioned by the topic as I developed commitments under their tutelage. My teachers are many, but I would like to point out one general category of teachers alongside two particular persons.

My first set of teachers were those who showed me what it means to lead a life that is prompted, motivated, and formed by the presence and work of the Spirit. Whether at a small group gathering at my childhood home in Hermosillo, Sonora, México or at a revivalist service at Timms Chapel in the woods close to Calhoun, Georgia, United States, I have seen, been touched by, and shaped in communities that one could describe as "gatherings in the Spirit." The running theme of these gatherings was that anybody—regardless of education, class, gender, race, or age—could be led and empowered by the Spirit to embody and show amazing, God-glorifying things. Early in my life, I intuitively sensed that there was something right about this claim as I saw it worked out and enfleshed by those around me. In my gut, I just knew this conviction was true and good. And looking back, I have increasingly realized just how beautiful those spaces, events, and people were. As I have transitioned in my life in terms of my location, work, and age, I have repeatedly reflected on these communities and experiences with fondness. This is a heritage of which to be proud, for it provided a priceless education.

My second set of teachers would be those who have taught me in formal academic settings. I have mentioned some of these people from time to time in my work. I would like to acknowledge particularly two professors who have taught me a great deal more than simply what and how to think. These would be Jackie and Cheryl Johns. I appreciate very much their willingness to take me under their wings during my seminary experience, and I consider them lifelong mentors and friends. It is particularly satisfying for me to dedicate this work to them because the Spirit shines through them in distinct and beautiful ways. Thank you, Cheryl, for reaching out to me and guiding me as a very young man. Thank you, Jackie, for your pastoral heart, humility, and wit.

dc
Seattle

In Memoriam: As I was finishing this text, a gunman opened fire at Seattle Pacific University on June 5, 2014, killing one student and injuring others in a hallway I have entered countless times. The one who died was Paul Lee, a student of mine who was exceptionally full of life and vitality, a "charismatic" figure to say the least. Without question, I have come to see the call of the teacher and the role of a learning community differently having gone through this experience. As for the theme of this book, I have become increasingly aware of the importance of narrating where and how the Spirit is at work in times of tragedy and loss, which in our case has repeatedly been in the embrace, care, and solidarity of those in our community during these very difficult circumstances. We have learned to be people of the Spirit in a distinct and profound way, all by the grace of God. With this experience, we join the fellowship of the suffering by yearning for that day when the New Jerusalem will come down—when God's Spirit, the Paraclete now and forever, will wipe every tear . . . and death will be no more.

PREFACE

Pneumatology—in this case the Christian theological sub-discipline devoted to the person and work of the Holy Spirit—is a deeply challenging field. Given the winds of Christian renewal sweeping across the globe today, perhaps no topic merits closer scrutiny and in turn has potential for wider application than this one within the field of Christian dogmatics. Despite this need, however, theologians, pastors, students, and laypeople continue to find themselves confused and frustrated with the topic. Easy, formulaic answers in pneumatology are simply unhelpful as circumstances and challenges unfold. Thoughtful, critical, and deeply earnest Christians continue to find the field puzzling, controversial, and maybe even unsettling. For these and other reasons, this book is needed, and if it can ameliorate this situation to some degree for some of its readers, it would have served its purpose.

The present book is not written so as to be an exhaustive reference work. One can find such books already on the market, some of which are quite helpful given their particular aims. If one stops to look at the bevy of books devoted exclusively to pneumatology, one can find a pattern among many of them: They often operate out of a methodological orientation that involves surveying the biblical materials, past figures and movements, and recent and contemporary thinkers and developments. Again, these works have their place. The difficulty with this methodological approach is that deeply complex movements and articulations are sometimes necessarily treated within the span of a few pages (or maybe just a couple of paragraphs). For readers who simply want a short, semi-encyclopedic approach to pneumatology, those works are worthwhile. But given that this approach is tried and worn, the present book attempts to do something different.

This text takes seriously as an orienting concern the words associated with the series of which it is a part: This book aims to be

a "guide" for readers who are genuinely "perplexed" by the topic
of God's Spirit in the field of Christian theology. It is a collection
of "working papers" (especially in its latter chapters) that offers a
glimpse into the field with the aim of clarifying some of the most
pressing concerns associated with it. Naturally, not all perplexities
can be addressed here. Repeatedly, I have found the task of writing
on this topic daunting simply because there is so much to clarify and
pursue. Quite simply, pneumatology needs much more development
than it has traditionally received. As I contemplated what themes
to pursue and how to approach them, I found myself gravitating to
certain concerns more so than others, and because of this tendency,
readers no doubt will find fault with some oversights that would
feature in more exhaustive studies. I can only say that among my
aims for the work comprehensiveness was not one of them.

The payoff with this text, as I see it, is not so much in terms
of coverage as in depth of exploration on some genuine concerns
within pneumatology. To go deep into a field one has to delve into
minutiae and particular concerns, and such is the case as one goes
on to specify challenges within it. The matter is further complicated
when such depth-registers involve moving forward amid a morass
of confusion and vying concerns. In my understanding, a "guide"
should not simply express the originating factors and conditions for
a "perplexing" situation but offer ways forward toward clarity and
semi-resolution. Therefore, the approach I have elected for myself
in the writing of this book involves by necessity a focus on only a
few areas of pneumatological inquiry, and in these I have tried to
elaborate what I see as the primary matters at stake within them and
constructive ways forward out of them. I find this orientation—with
the limits and possibilities it provides—to be unavoidable—at least
in terms of my own inclinations for writing a text such as this one.

Structurally, the work is subdivided into seven chapters.
Chapter 1 situates pneumatology within a broader set of challenges
and expectations. A key claim here is that people often find
pneumatology difficult because they have been conditioned to
approach the area on the basis of sensibilities and desires forged
within the realm of Christology. Once these can be identified and in
turn problematized so as to allow pneumatology to be taken on its
own terms, perhaps the field can explicitly be of increased service to
the faithful. Chapter 2 accounts for many of the dominant themes
in Spirit-talk found in the biblical witness. The tags, patterns,

phrases, and themes associated with the Spirit in Scripture form the linguistic and conceptual parameters and possibilities within the domain of this field. Part of the goal of this chapter is to register these—to put them on the table so to speak—since many of these will be picked up time and time again in what follows. But another purpose of the chapter is simply to show that Spirit-speech is a feature of the entire biblical witness and not simply of the New Testament. I have found (and treatments of Michael Welker's *God the Spirit* have repeatedly shown) that many Christians are simply unaware of the extent and shape of pneumatology within the whole of Christian Scripture. Readers, therefore, may find it worthwhile to see the gamut of Spirit-references within the whole of Scripture. Chapter 3 surveys the earliest construals of pneumatology within formal Christian reflection with an eye to the developments of the fourth century and on to the figure of Augustine. The controversial topic of the *filioque*—a matter of concern that has divided Roman Catholicism and Eastern Orthodoxy for centuries—will also be considered briefly here. Chapter 4 will treat of cosmological issues, particularly the relation between the Creator and creation as pneumatologically cast. On this front, the natural-supernatural divide will be questioned so that an interventionist model for understanding the Spirit's work is ultimately deemed inadequate to describe all that Christians wish to say about the Spirit's role within the cosmos. The topic of mediation is the focus of Chapter 5. Crucial to the life of the Christian community is the belief that the Spirit is at work in its midst through a variety of means provided by the triune God for the church's ongoing healing and sanctification. Features of that logic in addition to a particular treatment of Scripture will be offered. Chapter 6 will tackle a topic of vital concern for those cognizant of the milieu associated with Pentecostal and charismatic forms of Christianity; this issue is the question of Spirit-baptism particularly and the role of the Spirit in the ongoing maturation of believers. Partly at stake here is the "logic of subsequence" inherent to many pietist traditions. And finally, Chapter 7 will discuss the all-important question of discernment. Many Christians are especially keen to explore how one can identify and know the work of the Spirit in the contemporary situation. Certainly, no easy answers and no quick steps are available on this score, but a clearer sense of the complexity and range of issues involved can deepen forms of engagement with the theme.

Overall, this work attempts to make a case for why Spirit-talk is considerable on its own terms as a legitimate, vital, and necessary feature of Christian God-talk. For both theologians and laity alike, pneumatology has often been understood as something incidental or maybe even substantively unnecessary to Christian speech. One of the most oft-cited examples from the academic side to illustrate the point is Karl Barth. Eugene Rogers repeatedly finds that Barth announces the Spirit but goes on to expound the Son in his magisterial *Church Dogmatics*.[1] Whatever one makes of the intricate details of Rogers' assessment, the grounds for his orienting concern are self-evident: One repeatedly wonders where the Spirit has gone in Barth's proposals.[2] In contrast, Christians at the popular level often talk of "inviting Jesus into their hearts" with little to no explicit reference to the Spirit. Salvation, the Christian life, and many other themes as they are commonly treated by the laity are pneumatologically anemic. These and many more examples simply show that pneumatology is a field underdeveloped and underutilized in many contexts in which Christian speech is fostered so as to render an account of God and God's purposes in the world. This impoverishment needs remedying for all kinds of reasons, including the integrity of Trinitarian speech and the vitality and renewal of Christian existence. My desire with this work is that its readers can gain a greater appreciation and urgency for modifying at least their speech practices along pneumatological lines; if they do heed this call, they may in turn be surprised by what such kind of a shift could entail and ultimately trigger.

---

[1]See Eugene F. Rogers, *After the Spirit: A Constructive Pneumatology from Resources Outside the Modern West* (Grand Rapids, MI: Eerdmans, 2005), chapter 1.
[2]This to echo Robert W. Jenson, "You Wonder Where the Spirit Went," *Pro Ecclesia* 2 (1993): 296–304.

1

Facing the wind

Challenges and expectations within pneumatology

*"Nevertheless I tell you the truth: it is to your
advantage that I go away,
for if I do not go away, the Advocate will not come to you;
but if I go, I will send [this One] to you"*

JOHN 16:7

One of the most perplexing moments within the biblical testimony is when Jesus tells his disciples on the evening of his betrayal that they will actually *benefit* from his absence. Earlier in this section of John's Gospel (a section sometimes labeled the "Farewell Discourses," Chapters 14–17), Jesus made the link explicit between "another Advocate" and "the Spirit of truth, whom the world cannot receive, because it neither sees [this One] nor knows [this One]," but, according to Jesus, the disciples know this One because this One abides with them, and this One will be in them (John 14:16–18). Later in Chapter 14, Jesus makes much of the same gesture: "I have said these things to you while I am still with you. But the Advocate, the Holy Spirit, whom the Father will send in my name, will teach you everything, and remind you of all that I have said to you" (14:25–26; see also 15:26). When discussions of these passages ensue, often they take as their focus the many meanings that can be rendered from the word "Advocate" or *paraklētos* (sometimes transliterated as "Paraclete" in English); these possibilities include "representative," "counselor," and "comforter." These exegetical forays, however, do not reckon with the startling claim made by Jesus himself that the disciples would be at an advantage by his leaving. Would the contrasting corollary also hold, namely that the disciples would have been disadvantaged had Jesus remained with them? More to the point: What is the logic at work in this reasoning? What particular advantage does the Holy Spirit provide the disciples, one that apparently is unique to the Spirit?

Challenges of pneumatology

Before moving to speculate what these advantages could be, we should consider what sometimes people hold as the opposite view (at least implicitly), namely that the departure of Jesus and the coming of the Spirit are actually disadvantageous for believers. This view is often held because people generally find the study of Christ (Christology) much more helpful and available than the study of the Spirit (pneumatology). The mood is pithily captured by Eugene Rogers: Many Christians often think that "there's nothing the Spirit can do that the Son can't do better."[1] And people may hold this view because of the assumption, held by no less of a theologian than Wolfhart Pannenberg, that "there is almost no other subject in modern theology so difficult to deal with as the doctrine of the Holy Spirit is."[2] The perceived accessibility of Christology and the dumbfounding qualities associated with pneumatology make for a scenario where one will be privileged over the other. What might be some of the underlying factors for this current state of affairs, and when rigorously probed, are they ultimately compelling?

---

[1]Rogers explores the difficulties of this approach in *After the Spirit: A Constructive Pneumatology from Resources Outside the Modern West* (Grand Rapids, MI: Eerdmans, 2005), chapter 1.
[2]Wolfhart Pannenberg, "The Working of the Spirit in the Creation and in the People of God," in Wolfhart Pannenberg, Avery Dulles, and Carl Braaten (eds), *The Spirit, Faith, and the Church* (Philadelphia, PA: Westminster Press, 1970), p. 13.

Take for instance the most obvious reason why many people think Christology to be superior to pneumatology: Jesus was a living human being. Since we are humans, we tend to think that a natural bond exists between Jesus and us on the basis of our shared humanity. When the Bible speaks of Jesus sleeping, eating, walking, weeping, and so on, we can relate to those activities; he was a human with flesh and bones, just like we are. By way of contrast, Spirit-talk[3] is nebulous and difficult to pin down, and it is unclear how to make a connection between God's Spirit and us. Part of the difficulty, no doubt, relates to anthropological concerns. The following illustrates the challenge: Do humans have a spirit and/or a soul, or are they simply bodies and minds? In addition to anthropological questions, the broader category itself is unclear: The word "spirit" could mean any number of things, not just in terms of our own context but within the biblical world as well. In the Old Testament (OT), the word *ruach* can refer to breath, wind, entities that can in turn be morally evaluated (e.g. "evil spirits") pertaining to a "spiritual world," and internal aspects of both creatures (for instance, "the spirit of Elijah") and God's very self ("the Spirit of the LORD").[4] Additionally, the relevant word in Greek, *pneuma*, carries with it similar levels of indeterminate multiplicity: wind, human dispositions, a distinctive feature of God's identity and life—these are all possible renderings from the New Testament (NT) usage of *pneuma*. Therefore, *pneuma* is a fitting choice in the Septuagint to render the Hebrew word *ruach*; both words are similarly vague and open to multiple referents.

This form of indeterminacy surrounding such speech is difficult for Westerners to accommodate. One reason for this difficulty is the shape of Western intellectual history as it has been experienced in the contemporary era, for that tradition has experienced a sustained period of demythologization in which true knowledge is limited to a naturalized, empirical, material world. For many today, especially those in the Transatlantic North, a "spiritual world" is simply a

---

[3]Throughout this text, I use a number of constructions such as "Spirit-talk," "Spirit-speech," "Spirit-matters," and the like to communicate the linguistic and conceptual data that make up the field of Christian pneumatology.

[4]From Hebrew materials, the focus of this study will be on *ruach* and not on other possibilities such as *nephesh*, which can be rendered "soul," "life," or "life-force."

construct of prior, unenlightened peoples who ordered their lives on superstition and folklore. Talk of spirits alongside angels, demons, and the devil is simply a remnant of a bygone worldview, one that was necessarily superseded by a vision of reality that was deemed more consistent, reliable, testable, and generalizable. Although this tradition and its contemporary accoutrements are different from others across the globe (especially in regions collectively denominated as the "Global South"), for English-speaking domains, it almost goes without saying: A spirit-world is close to—if not altogether—an intellectual impossibility.

These circumstances create exceptional challenges for translators who are tasked with rendering very ancient literature and materials in ways that can be accessed by contemporary readers. Particularly within the domain of Spirit-talk and broadly in terms of allusions to spiritual realities, English translators of the Bible have often shown quite a bit of variety in the way they have gone about their work. Even in some cases, the typical reader would not know that the original term in question would be *ruach* or *pneuma* given translational prerogative.[5] Some cases where exceptional latitude has been exercised may be more understandable than others, but again, translators—at least on first blush—should be given some leeway in light of their formidable task of communicating in English what is so unwieldy for many contemporary hearers to appreciate both linguistically and conceptually.

Two particularly difficult aspects of translational work related to Spirit-talk that are significant for theological construction are capitalization and articular demarcation. For those who may not know, capitalization is a strict translational decision made in light of the biblical materials since the biblical manuscripts used to render modern-day translations do not exhibit decisions for or against capitalization. As for articular definition, there are cases in biblical Spirit-talk in which the explicit use of definite articles is available; in other cases, however, the definite article is not present but nevertheless possibly implied. On both counts, then, translators

---

[5]Take for example Proverbs 1:23, which is rendered by the NRSV as, "Give heed to my reproof; I will pour out my thoughts to you." The term "thoughts" is actually a form of *ruach* in Hebrew. Examples like this one suggest that Spirit-speech can be undetectable on the basis of translation alone.

are left with some difficult choices, and the decisions they do make
have a number of implications—including theological ones—
whether they consciously and intentionally recognize them or not.

Christians have typically wanted to capitalize and offer articular
definition when the referent of *ruach* or *pneuma* is judged to be the
Holy Spirit, that is, God's Spirit. One suspects Christians have engaged
in such activities not simply out of pious reverence but also in light
of the way they came to formulate their doctrine of God, which they
gradually took to mean as involving God's Spirit within God's self-
presentation as a unity-in-distinction.[6] Pneumatology, then, has usually
been understood as a field that has to do with the identity and work
of God's Spirit as Christians have come to understand such themes.
Broadly, this approach will also be the one assumed in the present
book, and that is why Spirit-references will typically be capitalized
since generally they will be understood (unless specifically stated) to
pertain to the Spirit of God. To repeat the point, pneumatology in this
book is understood as a sub-area within the doctrine of God.

This kind of specification, however, need not take away from the
recognition that the terms *ruach* and *pneuma* have a wide range
of application in the Bible and that their referents are sometimes
unclear. This last point is especially the case in which the interface
between God's Spirit and a "human spirit" is involved.[7] Given
certain people's commitments, the realm of pneumatology would
involve all the cases in which *ruach* and *pneuma* present themselves,
and with such a strategy, these scholars would wish to make a strong
(perhaps even conflationary) link between the divine and human
spirit.[8] After all, some passages simply lend themselves to multiple
readings because of their inherent ambiguity.

---

[6]See Geoffrey Wainwright, "The Holy Spirit," in Colin E. Gunton (ed.), *The
Cambridge Companion to Christian Doctrine* (Cambridge: Cambridge University
Press, 1997), p. 273.
[7]Recall the examples of both Moses in Numbers 11 and Elijah in 2 Kings 2. In both
cases, the spirit in them is referred to as individually theirs and yet the effects and
workings of their spirits suggest something more than simply an anthropological
category. Potential ambiguous examples from the NT are Luke 1:80; 1 Corinthians
14:32; and James 4:5.
[8]Of course, this tendency is found in Idealism as well as random proposals found
throughout the theological academy. This approach will be resisted in the present
book because of the havoc it wreaks on a doctrine of creation specifically and the
theological character of dogmatics on the whole.

In response to this expansive strategy towards pneumatology, let me say the following. No doubt, given the challenges involved, translators and interpreters bring much of themselves to the process of rendering judgments regarding how best to relate the many instances of *ruach* and *pneuma*. These factors not only involve textual but also worldview-related (and so theological) concerns. For this reason, these judgments and renderings should be tested and probed by any serious student of pneumatology and so not taken simply at face value as they are presented in any particular translation of the Bible. Furthermore, the background commitments at play for translator and reader alike should be identified to the degree possible, which is oftentimes quite difficult since these are rarely brought to the fore for evaluation and negotiation. In the case of this volume, the doctrine of creation—as a mechanism for preserving a dialectical relationship between the Spirit's nearness and vastness—proves crucial, and its range of significance will be pursued in a subsequent chapter.

For the sake of clarity, let me say here: I find the biblical materials to suggest an array of distinctions between God's Spirit and other spirit-phenomena (human spirits, evil spirits, the wind, and so on), even if the same terms are used to denominate all of them. As appropriate as some scholars have been in pushing against the tendency to offer rushed delineations in such cases, I believe the point still stands that there is a distinction to be maintained particularly along the lines of the Creator-creation interface. That the same words (*ruach* and *pneuma*) can be appropriated in such varied ways need not mean that they are referring to the same thing. The analogous nature of God-talk presents itself once more as it does in all cases in which the same terms are used in service of describing the Creator and the creation. God's Spirit and a human spirit are not necessarily unrelated matters (univocity), but given the agents involved, it is worth noting also that they are markedly different (equivocity).

The challenges of pneumatology continue not only at the level of language and translation but also in terms of relationality. Typically, Christians feel more at ease in relating to Jesus than they do to the Spirit. Why? Jesus was a personal entity. He had a name, personality, and heritage. He was a son, teacher, carpenter, and friend. We can relate to Jesus on the basis of such demarcations and characteristics since these are part of the human experience that frames everything we are and know. In contrast, how does one relate to God's Spirit? Can one address or speak to the Spirit? Broadly, should God's Spirit be thought of in personal terms?[9] These and many other questions are difficult for contemporary Christians to pursue because of their epistemic frameworks, but interestingly, Spirit-talk has always had a degree of relational difficulty associated with it. As it will be noted below, concerted formulation of Christian pneumatology within the church took place after quite a bit of efforts were pursued in Christology. Additionally, there were various stages of pneumatological development, and these emerged from and interacted with both Jewish formulations as well as a number of eventually deemed heretical sensibilities and movements. All of this to say that the early church struggled with precisely this line of inquiry for centuries, and it did so with very good reason. When some refer to the Spirit as the "shy member of the Trinity," part of the warrant for such a description relies on difficulties in categorizing the Holy Spirit in personal terms.

The language of John's gospel (which will serve as a guiding refrain in this book) as well as many instances elsewhere in the NT and across Christian tradition would suggest that the Holy Spirit is an entity who is distinctly identifiable and who engages in specific activities, including relating to, guiding, and reminding Christ's disciples. In other words, on this account the Spirit appears to be hypostatically personal. Part of the rationale for this judgment is that Jesus spoke of the Spirit as "another Paraclete," which by implication suggests that the Spirit is an entity similar to Christ, the forerunning *paraklētos*. On the basis of this understanding, the matter would seem to be settled—the Spirit is personal like Jesus. And yet, Scripture complicates this uniform presentation.

For instance, the Spirit is also portrayed in Scripture as a power or presence that comes upon or is mediated via some other agent. As illustrative of this possibility, consider the following: A typical biblical pattern is that God's Spirit comes, rests, rushes upon, or fills a person, and *that person* goes on to speak or act in distinct ways. Jesus himself spoke of the Spirit as being *in* the disciples,

[9]For a very helpful discussion of this question, see Bernd Oberdorfer, "The Holy Spirit—A Person?," in Michael Welker (ed.), *The Work of the Spirit* (Grand Rapids, MI: Eerdmans, 2006), pp. 27–46.

a claim suggesting that the work of the Spirit would be through them—that is mediated via their speech and activity. Put another way, one can hear and read the words of Jesus in the gospels,[10] but where are the Spirit's voice and words to be found apart from the voice and words of others? The thrust of these questions points toward the recognition that the Spirit works in and through creaturely contingencies and means.[11] Of course, Jesus' voice and words are mediated through the gospel writers, but this kind of mediation is on the basis of what they had heard, seen, and touched concerning the word of life in the flesh (cf. 1 John 1). The mediation involved with the Spirit is of a different order. In this case, Christ's disciples necessarily experience the Spirit differently, not in terms of the "Spirit's flesh" per se but through others' bodies, through the sacramental activities of faith communities—in short through a larger dynamic involving the Spirit's manifold self-presentation and work within the community of the faithful, that is the church.

With this kind of fluidity at play, the historical and contextual boundaries and restraints are less pronounced. As a result, questions present themselves, particularly of an epistemological variety so that one genuinely wonders how one can know the Spirit's presence and work. Despite these formidable challenges, Christians were bold enough to speak of the Spirit in personal ways because of certain prompts in Scripture and also because of the Trinitarian commitments they developed over time. The latter were deeply contested and took

---

[10]And without question, despite the difficulty of some to recognize the point at the popular level, this form of divine self-disclosure involved mediation as well. The incarnation represents God's mediated word par excellence. I would stress that perceiving and knowing the things of God necessarily involves a kind of Trinity-enabled empiricism. Yes, Jesus said and did things, but their proper perception pushes into greater complexity on the epistemological front than many would care to admit. Put another way, neglect of the Spirit is often due to an unworkable Christology. The point will be registered further below.

[11]A few instances in the NT may be taken to challenge this point because the Spirit is said to have spoken (Acts 13:2) or told people to go to or avoid certain places and activities (see, for instance, Acts 16:6–7; 20:23; 21:24), as if these are somehow "directly" known from the Spirit in an unmediated way. These cases are usually brought up in passing, so it is impossible to know all that is involved with each. Nevertheless, the deliberative happenings that led up to the Jerusalem Council claiming "it has seemed good to the Holy Spirit and to us" (Acts 15:28) as well as the case of Agabus directly warning Paul about going to Jerusalem (Acts 21:10–11) both show in fuller ways how the Spirit goes about working in the world.

some time to develop especially after the Council of Nicaea, which shows once again how pneumatology has specific challenges that distinguish it from Christology and yet the development of both have historically taken place in close proximity at certain important junctures. The present work will assume this tradition of casting the Spirit in personal terms; however, this move will be executed with great caution since plenty instances of Spirit-talk in the Bible (especially in the Old Testament) suggest something other than this hypostatizing vision for the Spirit's "self." Therefore, the Spirit can be understood as personal so that a connection can be understood to exist between the Spirit and creatures, but the Spirit should also be understood as "transpersonal" in a certain kind of way. One of the outcomes from thinking of the Spirit as personal is that the Spirit can be addressed akin to an "I-Thou" framework; however, the "Thou" in question knows us more profoundly than we know ourselves and is One who helps us in our weakness with groans too deep for words (Rom 8:26). Therefore the Spirit is a special kind of "Thou"—One who also mysteriously occupies important registers of both the "I" as well as the "dash" of such a formulation. To neglect this feature of Spirit-talk would be to diminish important contributions that pneumatology could make both to theological endeavoring and the life of piety.

The transpersonal nature of the Spirit has implications for another major challenge within the field of pneumatology. This particular matter involves both language and personhood/relationality; the issue would be gender. When people think of the words (and on Trinitarian grounds, one can say "names") "Father" and "Son," an ease with pronouns and imagery naturally follows. Perhaps people feel comfortable using male pronouns in association with God in part because grammatically one would need to use them for these two Trinitarian persons. One properly speaks of the Father and Jesus in terms of a "he," so why not speak of God and God's Spirit as a "he" as well? More generally—and perhaps more predominantly—people at the popular level often associate God-qualities with what are deemed to be male qualities (and vice versa). Such is especially the case with the privileging of such attributes as omnipotence and sovereignty. Problems exist all around for these kinds of construals, but they are nevertheless made with startling and steady frequency. God's nature and whatever is deemed as "maleness" have and continue to be associated with one another in Western culture. For many people, the alternative is untenable: the association of God with "female characteristics" sounds not only inappropriate but also religiously pagan (and so anti-Christian).

Quite a few matters and corresponding claims are involved in these determinations, so many in fact that they cannot be treated adequately here. In terms of pneumatology, the case is not clear at all; it certainly is not as easy as it would seem when speaking of the Father and the Son. Should one speak of the Spirit in male terms? For some, the answer is a resounding "yes." Reasons in support of this move involve consistency with other Trinitarian speech practices, prior commitments related to the God-gender question, and possibly a host of others. Rather than brushing the matter aside, it certainly is worth pondering, for arguably this is but another dimension of Spirit-talk that could contribute uniquely and generatively to the theological enterprise.

The case of English speakers is especially noteworthy as illustrative of the difficulty. As prevalent as the tendency is to speak of the Spirit in male terms in English, no convincing reason exists for exhaustively doing so.[12] In other words, Spirit-language in English is not any more male than female, and so the gender constraints associated with the words "Father" and "Son" do not apply in the case of the Spirit on grammatical grounds. Others, wishing for antecedence on this matter, may be inclined to look to ancient languages (particularly those of importance for Christian history) for help. What they find from such endeavoring, however, is also inconclusive. Unlike English, many languages have gender associated with nouns as a matter of grammatical consequence, but on this score, as Jerome found particularly interesting, one can see the gamut of possibilities expressed: *ruach* in Hebrew is typically in feminine form, *pneuma* in Greek is neuter, and *spiritus* in Latin is masculine. Because English does not have this grammatical feature to nouns, the use of personal pronouns in Spirit-talk in English is a decision English speakers make with little grammatical warrants for what they ultimately decide. Once again, the interpretive, judgment-based dimensions inherent to pneumatology come to the fore, now in terms of gender specificity.

---

[12]One possible exception here is *paraklētos*: This term is masculine in Greek but it is one title given to the Spirit only in John's gospel. This sole example should not be taken as settling the gender question in pneumatology once and for all.

Students of pneumatology should bear in mind that the question of gender is not simply grammatical; it is of theological consequence as well. Therefore, whatever is chosen on this front will necessarily be impactful, not simply in terms of readers' sensibilities but also in relation to an ongoing account and vision of who God must be and how God must be like. How will this text tackle this dynamic? As problematic as it is to do so, this work will refer to the Spirit in neuter and gender-neutral terms. This decision is based on several important factors. To rehearse the claim above, no good grammatical reason exists to privilege male terms in Spirit-talk. The convention of past English speakers is simply not sufficient given the stakes involved with this matter. Given the grammatical consequences involved with the names of "Father" and "Son," at some level it is proper to refer to these persons in male terms; however, the same restraints do not hold for the Spirit. In other words, the Spirit need not be spoken of in male terms, and this kind of possibility, I contend, should be utilized in light of what is typically done on grammatical grounds for the Father and the Son.

Most believers will recognize that sex and gender are characteristics of creaturehood and not divinity. Humans are like God because they stem from God, yet "God is not a human being" (Num 23:19). Part of what it typically has meant to be human is to be sexed and gendered, whereas most Christians have found it implausible to view God's life as sexed and gendered since these involve inhabiting a body, which in turn is narrated and constructed in a certain way. In short, there is a certain impropriety involved in calling the Christian God a "he," and yet that affirmation may lose some force with the Trinitarian language of "Father" and "Son" (registered formally through the words of Jesus as communicated through the gospel testimony). The choice of neuter and gender-neutral language is a way of expressing more closely through linguistic forms what is believed to be true at the conceptual level of God's life *in se*.

If male terms are problematic and yet deemed indispensable (given Jesus' life and speech practices), then why not employ feminine terms for the Spirit as a counterbalancing act? In response, such a strategy would be problematic from the other side of the gender-dynamic. God's Spirit does not have a body, so female terms (just as male ones) do not apply. The choice of female pronouns for the Spirit so as to allegedly balance gender distribution within God-talk is an unclear motive. First of all, it is not obvious what a "balance" would even look like and if it is even possible given (to put the matter grossly) the two-to-one ratio involved. But more importantly, feminine pronouns for the Spirit functionally keep the male-female dyad as primordial in God-talk, and that is ultimately the real difficulty to overcome.[13] Therefore, the use of feminine terms for the Spirit may in the long term undermine the motives one has for doing so by embedding further gender specification within the Godhead.

With male and female possibilities off the table for Spirit-talk, one is left by a process of elimination with neuter and gender-neutral terms. I recognize that following this strategy may result in unconventional and cumbersome prose, and a potential risk with such a move is that it may be taken by readers as mischaracterizing and depersonalizing the Spirit. My response to this worry: As my editors are prone to tell me, my prose may be difficult no matter what, even with feminine terms included for the Spirit. But more seriously, depersonalization in Spirit-talk is not necessarily a bad thing given the above claims registered about the Spirit's transpersonal self. To specify further: I try to avoid using the language of "it" for the Spirit, but I will typically refer to the Spirit through titles, a range of names, and the personal yet gender-generic (and capitalized) option of "One."

When taken as a whole, these challenges in pneumatology point to a running motif within the field: Christian commitments about the Spirit tend to defy many of the categories and designations we use to make sense of our reality and environment. In particular, Spirit-speech pushes up against the many binaries or dyads that we often use to narrate ourselves and our world. Think of the many cases where dyadic thinking presses upon our conceptual commitments and imaginations: Material or immaterial, natural or supernatural, personal or impersonal, God or cosmos, Creator or creation, male or female, Jew or Gentile, the rich or the poor, black or white, up or down, old or new—the list could be extended endlessly. The Spirit is not constrained by these stratifications of reality even though our speech and thought patterns often are. And frankly, these constraints are not neutral since they miss so much variability and complexity in

[13]For more on this point, see Sarah A. Coakley, "The Trinity and Gender Reconsidered," in Miroslav Volf and Michael Welker (eds), *God's Life in Trinity* (Minneapolis: Fortress Press, 2006), pp. 133–42.

their wake. In fact, part of Christianity's pneumatological heritage is that the Spirit actively works against these constructions and categories for the sake of showing an alternative reality, one that is characterized by the Christian belief in the One who is making *all things* new (cf. Rev 21:5). Put another way, when pursued in a certain way, pneumatology can alter our imaginary to the core by calling into question the neat categories—usually in terms of binaries, dyads, or couplets—we use to order ourselves and our world. Such work is useful and maybe even necessary to account for greater degrees of complexity, subtlety, depth, and meaningfulness within the Christian way of participating in the world.

Recalibrating expectations

These many layers of complexity may overwhelm those who desire pneumatology to have the same form of concretization that Christology has. From one perspective, pneumatology would not be so perplexing if it were as available, conceptually and practically, as Christology. Nevertheless, much could be said to problematize the assumed ease with which Christology may be understood, and this problematization has consequences not only for Christology but pneumatology as well. A reframing of expectations may be in order so that one can come to see the distinct contribution the Spirit makes to the Christian way of life. This contribution is meaningful and important, but it is only perceivable once one allows for a reformulation of theological desiderata, particularly if these have been shaped and reified along Christological lines.

To begin this reordering of expectations, one can pick up some of the themes that were already registered above. The act of speaking of God—of describing and characterizing God as one confesses God—is one that involves language, and language as such is at its core a limited vehicle for expressing the faith's holy mysteries. With an intuited sense of God's manifest glory, one cannot help but recognize how words have to break down in some way when put to use to describe God. Words simply cannot contain and communicate God's splendor. Quite the contrary, as necessary as words are, they may complicate and even corrupt the apprehension of the Holy One of Israel. Scripture itself recognizes this difficulty surrounding

God-talk and offers its readers multitudinous ways to speak of God, ones that have been brought together at times through the mechanism of dialectic. When one ventures to speak of God in light of the prompts of Scripture so that one goes on to say that God is loving and wrathful, merciful and just, immovable and responsive, what becomes clear is that God reveals Godself in ways that break down under their own generative pressure. For instance, Scripture characterizes God as a mother-hen, a mighty warrior, living water, a still small voice, and so on. The school that is Holy Writ teaches its readers to be versatile and nimble in the ways they go on to speak of the God revealed in its pages. Because of this diversity, theologians at different times and places have opted to consider the apophatic dimension of Christian speech—that words have to be affirmed and voided, and through such a process something more conceptually fitting for God can be apprehended and communicated.

Unfortunately, this guiding sensibility of the limits of language for communicating holy mysteries is rarely explicitly recognized within the domain of Christology. Quite simply, Christ is often understood to be readily—and one might even say, excessively— available by rank and file Christians in the way they participate in the faith. Take for instance the number and variety of Jesus-depictions one can easily find. In addition to their proper and reverent employment in holy icons, depictions of Christ are readily found on T-shirts, bookmarks, signs, magazine covers, and so on. Artwork of Jesus across the globe often takes the dominant ethnic forms and characteristics of the cultures in which it arises. Such developments are understandable and fitting to some degree. After all, Christ is "God with us" as one of us; therefore, these depictions can be expressions of the solidarity Christians feel they have been shown through Jesus because of their belief that God has come in the flesh to be one of them. However, as fitting as these expressions may be, one has to wonder when the dangers of projectionism and domestication set in. All God-talk has to resist the threats of sentimentalization and cultural absorption, and these have proven especially difficult to avoid in Christology.

Alternatively, the Spirit is less circumscribable to depicted and localized forms, and whereas some may find this a difficulty in terms of relating to this One, this quality certainly may function to hold at bay projectionist (and merchandizing!) tendencies. Of course, people can also domesticate the Spirit through their speech and thought. Some Christians do this by claiming to "have the Spirit" in ways others do not—as if the Spirit were their exclusive possession. Examples like this show that the corruption of God-talk is difficult to avoid when the power of language and the employment of thought forms go unchecked and are registered casually and uncritically. Without some kind of vigilant, communal self-monitoring, God-talk can easily be abused and manipulated for unfaithful and maybe even sinful ends. Having recognized these possibilities, however, one can go on to see that the Spirit's defiance of concretization and particularization—at least at some level—can help resist the clutches of objectification and commodification in God-talk since Spirit-speakers have to face head-on the limits of language in their specific kind of theological endeavoring. Because of the Spirit's nature, it is very difficult to imagine putting a face to the Spirit, of depicting the Spirit in some concretized form. Again, options are available in Scripture (a dove, fire, wind, and so on), but these are not necessarily popular or easy to render. After all, how would a person draw or paint something like breath? By working through the ambiguity and indeterminacy of Spirit-talk in the Bible, one necessarily brushes up against the limits of language in God-talk, and by doing so, one can foster and cultivate certain sensibilities that can contribute to the faithful and nuanced pursuit of theological endeavoring overall. Put another way, by working through the field of pneumatology one can learn how to more faithfully render God-talk in a way that expresses and is guided by some of the limitations inherent to such endeavoring generally.

Furthermore, as advantageous as it would seem to have "God in the flesh" before one's eyes, not all people across space and time could have such an experience since a human being is bound by such limits. Jesus only came into contact with a relatively few amount of people in his lifetime, and the act of taking on human flesh this side of the fall meant that he at some point or another was going to die just as all of us will. In short, access to Jesus—the "enfleshed" God—reckons with a number of historical and bodily constraints. Involved with these limits would be the many ways people could respond to Jesus upon encountering him: Some could listen, obey, and follow him; others could hurt, assault, and kill him. The advantages associated with Jesus, then, could be portrayed from another angle as significant difficulties for a God who has come unto God's own as one of them.

By way of contrast, these limits are not ones that immediately apply to an "inspirited" God, so to speak. Unlike the limits of a body, God's Spirit can move and work across time and space. What typically are associated as limitations for God's self-presentation in Jesus do not apply to the Spirit of YHWH. This kind of expansiveness and freedom is a sign of sheer grace: No matter their circumstances or location, Christians operate with the hope that they can call on the name of God, and not only does God listen to them but God is also truly and always present with them wherever they are.[14] God can be for the world in this way because "God is spirit" (John 4:24). The Spirit of God, unlike "God in the flesh," cannot be killed. Quite the contrary, this spirit is the Spirit of life and resurrection, the One who resolutely raised Jesus from the dead as a sign of God's inbreaking reign and victory over all sin and death.

Finally (and as noted previously), speaking of the Spirit can challenge the typical male language often used for God in theological speech. Given that God is the creator of both men and women and that men and women can only relate to God within the parameters of their embodied selves, pneumatology can be particularly liberating, especially when contrasted with Christology. From the side of the latter, Jesus was obviously in the flesh as a man. He spoke of the God of the ancestors in terms of his "Father." These forms of concretization potentially can come at a significant cost. They may inspire men to think that they resemble or have a closer connection with God strictly on the basis of their sex, and women may have difficulty relating to an incarnate God who is presented to them in exclusively masculine terms, especially if they have suffered abuse or discrimination at the hands of men. Both men and women need to wrestle with the claim that Jesus was not so much the "God-man" as the "God-human," but this kind of endeavoring is quite difficult to sustain given the concrete, undeniable particularities associated with Jesus' life. After all, Jesus enjoyed privileges and opportunities in his first-century context simply because he was a male; he could go to certain places and interact with particular people given the

---

[14]In this sense, the claim Jesus makes of being with his disciples "unto the end of the age" (Matt 28:20) is thoroughly a pneumatologically inflected prospect. The Spirit has *always* been part of the Son's self-presentation, be it in earthly or resurrected and ascended flesh.

advantages his gender granted him within his first-century milieu. Although taking different forms no doubt, patriarchy was alive and well in Jesus' day as it is in ours. By way of promise, pneumatology may be the church's most helpful dogmatic resource is countering patriarchy and its ill-effects, including those deemed (rightfully or wrongfully) to be directly tied to Christological forms and consequences.

A field of exceptional promise

As noted earlier, the Spirit defies the easy categorizations that we use to order our reality, including—and perhaps most especially— the dyadic stratification of reality. Rather than privileging whatever God-forms can easily fit into these prevalent categories, theological speakers would do well to maintain a modicum of humility by recognizing that what may be conceptually easy or familiar may at the end of the day complicate or inhibit the ability to see what the Spirit is doing or beckoning of the faithful. The Holy Spirit is oftentimes at the margins or just outside of the limelight while raising leaders, empowering witnesses, and comforting the lowly. What may appear strange or out of place may on second glance be something that has its source in the Spirit's prompting and timely presence. These many claims are not suggesting chaos and disorder; quite the contrary, the Spirit is orderly and intentional in the Spirit's workings. As many Roman Catholic scholars (especially those sympathetic to the charismatic renewal) are willing to admit, the charismatic and institutional features of ecclesial life can coexist and complement one another.[15] Therefore, as difficult as the field may be, perhaps no field of theological study is more necessary and promising than pneumatology is today.

The church has always faced a number of challenges in maintaining a vital witness. These challenges have oftentimes been in relation to divisions of all kinds. Classism, ageism, racism, sexism, ableism—these and many more work against the unity to which Christians are called. The Spirit works outside and inside the

---

[15]This possibility is masterfully demonstrated in Yves Congar, *I Believe in the Holy Spirit* (New York: Crossroad, 2000).

barriers erected by humans and in turn subverts these obstructions so as to show glimpses and first-fruits of God's reign. Take for instance the role of women in Christian gatherings. Whereas most societies have succumbed to one form of patriarchy or another, revivalist movements with strong Spirit-emphases have oftentimes granted greater roles for women in their communal arrangements. This kind of involvement is not recent, for those in the Society of Friends—a pneumatological movement if there ever was one—were welcoming women's participation in their meetings in the seventeenth century. A number of women also came to prominence in the nineteenth-century Holiness Movement. A major figure here was Phoebe Palmer, who was able to justify her role as a Christian leader on the basis of "the promise of the Father" (Acts 1:4), the baptism of the Holy Spirit. This logic was predicated upon the happenings of Acts 2, particularly Peter's citation of Joel's prophecy in which sons *and daughters* will prophesy. These are just some instances from Christian history in which pneumatology and the freeing of the marginalized have coalesced. Today, a number of Spirit-movements are not only promoting religious fervor but also actively pursuing structural social change throughout the world.[16] The Spirit quickens and charges the community of the faithful in hopeful, imaginative ways. Rather than being an excuse to participate in a privatized spirituality, emphases on the Spirit can actually ready a Christian community to be more engaged with the ills that confront it both from within and without.

Looking ahead

To conclude this chapter and to anticipate those that follow, one can say pneumatology is a field of exceptional promise with a rich history of reflection in Christian theology. Its importance extends particularly to the matters above and generally to the grand Christian vision involving both God and the life made possible by God. Once one allows for one's expectations to be recalibrated and re-narrated in light of the biblical, historical, and theological

---

[16]On this front, see Donald E. Miller and Tetsunao Yamamori, *Global Pentecostalism* (Berkeley: University of California, 2007).

resources at the church's disposal, the pursuit of pneumatology can illuminate and foster key possibilities within the theological task and thus substantiate the pursuit of the Christian way of life. As sad as certain words and moments are in John's "Farewell Discourses," another side to the story exists: Christians have not been left alone. Jesus promises that the Spirit of truth will lead and guide them into all things since this One is with and in them. This One is the Spirit of resurrection, and because of who this One is, this vision is truly hopeful, empowering, emboldening, and comforting for Christians today. As Bishop Kallistos Ware has remarked, the call of the Christian is to be nothing short of a Spirit-bearer.[17] In heeding this call, Christians can lead a truly humanizing existence, one that draws its strength, hope, and character from the Trinity who is exceedingly and wonderfully for us by being Immanuel—God with us—in flesh *and* spirit.

---

[17]Kallistos Ware, *The Orthodox Way* (Crestwood, NY: St. Vladimir's Seminary Press, 1979), p. 90.

2

The shape of Spirit-talk

Biblical tags, patterns, and themes

"The words that I have spoken to you are spirit and life"
JOHN 6:63

When Spirit-talk is surveyed in terms of the biblical materials, one first has to recognize that different voices, books, canonical units, and epochs within the Bible itself render a number of distinct wordings and patterns. Again, some may find this level of variety—now in terms of Scripture—to be off-putting since the expectation might be that the Bible—despite its many centuries of composition, compilation, and transmission—should communicate a singular vision for the identity and work of God's Spirit. In the eyes of many, the Bible reflects God's self-communication, and this form of divine self-disclosure presumably should be consistent and coherent. Unfortunately, some find consistency and coherence to be synonymous with uniformity and homogeneity. This move, however, is disputable at a number of levels. Diversity and plurality are not necessarily threats to truth and meaning any more than consistency and invariability. God's Spirit can operate in surprising ways without such activity being deemed necessarily erratic or innovative. The manifold character of the Spirit's operations can be embraced without the assumption of its eventual dissolution into willy-nilly nonsense. Truth and meaning are simply more expansive than any construct can accommodate, including single formulations of what "consistency" and "coherence" look like and how they can be apprehended. The diversity of Spirit-talk within the Bible—rather than an impediment to be overcome—can be conceived as a gift to the church in the sundry conditions in which it finds itself; of course, that conceptualization relies on not simply the perspicacity of Scripture but also, among other things, the hermeneutical pliability of the reading community as well.

In the following, a number of examples of Spirit-talk from the Bible will be considered. Admittedly, one chapter cannot do justice to the gamut of images and ideas of the Spirit found in Scripture. Whole books barely can account for all the cases involved, much less, then, can a single chapter do so. For those books that do treat these materials in some exhaustive kind of way, their methodological tendency usually is to survey passages, biblical books, or units in an orderly way with the goal of proving an overarching thesis. To some degree, this strategy is unavoidable, and this chapter will proceed with the survey approach with the accompanying claim of not striving after exhaustiveness. The distinctiveness of the following presentation is that Scripture passages will be surveyed largely in terms of indeterminate tags, patterns, and themes so as to register them for subsequent dogmatic consideration and appropriation.

The use of terms such as "tags" and "codings" in what follows is for the representation of linguistic forms people use from the scriptural testimony in their dogmatic reflection that are not entirely clear within their original contexts as to their determinate meaning. They are tropes that become registered in the parlance of the Christian church, but the way they are picked up and substantiated varies from fellowship to fellowship.[1] A prominent example of such a tag would be "Spirit-baptism." This coding is derivable from Scripture, but its referent—what the tag is actually describing, its *res* so to speak—and all of its registers and implications are altogether unclear from the Bible's single witness. For clarity and a working sense of

[1]This varying usage is ordered by what I have elsewhere called "primordial log-ics" or "Ur-commitments." See Daniel Castelo, "The Spirit, Creaturehood and Sanctification," *International Journal of Systematic Theology* 16.2 (2014): 177–91.

such tropes, a reading community has to come along and fill in the gaps, so to speak. Given this process, diversity will naturally ensue from the wide range of factors involved.[2] So, yes, John the Baptist proclaims Jesus will "baptize in the Spirit." Undoubtedly, this is a feature of the Baptist's message. However, what does this phrase actually mean, and how can its meaning take shape in everyday life? As readers of the gospels become acquainted with the life, words, and ministry of Jesus, they are tasked with making sense of how to interconnect John's proclamation with the shape of Jesus' life and ministry. Quite simply, the phrasing itself—as important as it is—retains a level of ambiguity throughout the gospel presentation. Communities of interpretation necessarily go on to provide the logics necessary to make such codings come to life for people at the ground level of living. The particular topic of Spirit-baptism will be considered extensively in a subsequent chapter of this book, but it is mentioned here to illustrate a broader point surrounding not only pneumatology but dogmatics generally: Certain fellowships pick up a word or phrase and use it quite differently from its appropriation by other such groups; therefore, people may use the same tag to refer to distinct, separate realities. When this scenario plays out, the situation can become quite muddled rather quickly, a development which may unsettle some observers but one that is naturally tied to the complexity surrounding the practice of biblical interpretation and theological construction.

As for "patterns" and "themes," the Bible does regularly show across its many books and units some large-scale similarities or correlations in Spirit-speech. In terms of patterns, one can note, for instance, how the Spirit comes upon a number of prophets, judges, and kings at specific moments in their lives for particular ends or purposes. These patterns are crucial to identify as one makes headway in considering the Spirit's work across the biblical testimony and tries in turn to offer a broad account of the Spirit's activity across the biblical literature. In this process, some themes will naturally come to the fore that may not be widely distributed among the biblical materials but are nevertheless important to

---

[2]Amos Yong's trialectical vision is helpful here; see *Spirit-Word-Community: Theological Hermeneutics in Trinitarian Perspective* (Eugene, OR: Wipf and Stock, 2002).

consider given their prominence in Christian reflection on the Spirit. For instance, Lukan and Pauline pneumatologies are sometimes differentiated on the basis of recurring themes in their respective contributions.

Overall, the goal of the present chapter is to communicate a working sense of some of the most important pneumatological features of the biblical testimony, a witness that inflects the grammar and shape of Christian speech and existence since it is itself an auxiliary of the Holy Spirit that is aimed at forming a mature Christian ethos.[3]

Old Testament

Outside of certain places in the prophetic literature, Christians may not know the extent of Spirit-talk in the OT, but interestingly, quite a few examples and themes are available from this part of the Bible that pertain to the topic. Biblical scholars and theologians have been aware of these materials, but sometimes they have not been sure what to do with them. Scholars have worried about the ease with which Christians "read into" the OT their own constructs and understandings so that in terms of pneumatology, scholars have demonstrated concern with the penchant Christians have historically shown to read Spirit-texts of the OT from the lens of fourth-century Trinitarian commitments. For Christians, the Spirit came to be understood as a person of the Trinity who eternally subsists within the triune life of the Christian God. Obviously, reading OT Spirit-texts from this vantage point could appear anachronistic to those who take a predominantly historicist point of view. In registering this concern, these scholars would be worried that the Bible is just an occasion by which to express Christian commitments that are formed independently of the text and so imposed upon it at will, making the reading of the Bible something untethered from some kind of objective realism that could stand over and against such commitments. As a dogmatician, my tendencies lean toward a theological reading of Scripture without downplaying some historical

---

[3] I owe the language of "auxiliary" in this case to my colleague Robert W. Wall.

account of the biblical materials.[4] But then again, "history" is not anymore of a neutral category than "reason" is. The locating of Scripture within the economy of God's purposes, therefore, challenges easy bifurcations between theology and history. The interpretation of certain key texts can help show how such work can feel like one is wading through a contentious, methodological landmine.

Take, for instance, the plurals one detects in moments of God's speaking in the OT—most notably the case of "let us make humankind in our image" in Genesis 1:26. For some Christian interpreters, these instances are taken as the earliest biblical signs of Trinitarianism. Grammatically, the plural within the word *Elohim* in Hebrew is responsible for this case, and eager Christians seeking for biblical support for the doctrine of the Trinity may see this example as simply too good to pass up in their desire to see Trinitarianism exhibited within OT materials. Of course, many readers of this text could point to other reasons for this form (for instance, it could be a divine/royal plural), and naturally, writers and readers at the time of Genesis' composition and compilation would not have had Trinitarianism in mind. Therefore, a methodological tension is at play as to how one goes about making sense of this particular form of expression.

Valid reasons exist for methodological diversity in biblical interpretation. Certainly, texts have to be contextualized in their many aspects; otherwise, the Bible loses its integrity as a genuine witness to the self-presentation of the God of Christian worship within time and space. Contextualization involves all kinds of concerns, including historical, cultural, social, linguistic, and literary factors. At the same time, from their earliest beginnings, Christians have appropriated and appealed to the OT in ways that demonstrated their deepest Christian commitments. The way the Servant Songs of Isaiah are alluded to in the canonical gospels, for instance, is one important example of this tendency. These passages have their distinct contextual resonances, but they are also picked up within the Christian imaginary in important ways, and this last move is legitimate on the faith commitment that all of Scripture is a testament to the self-presentation of the triune God of Christian confession. Therefore, *biblical* precedent exists

---

[4]For my approach to this unwieldy feature involved in biblical interpretation, see Bo H. Lim and Daniel Castelo, *Hosea*, Two Horizons Old Testament Commentary Series (Grand Rapids, MI: Eerdmans, forthcoming), chapter 1.

for reading the OT through the Christian worldview; this is simply a dynamic pertaining to a two-testament canon as it has come to us as Christian readers.

In light of these concerns, how is a Christian to navigate the terrain of Spirit-talk in the OT? One way is simply to account for the many instances of *ruach* in the OT and allow for these to stand in their distinct and collective complexity and ambiguity. That gesture in itself creates some hermeneutical differentiation, for as noted in the previous chapter, the term *ruach* can mean much more than simply "spirit." And yet determination and specification cannot be deferred perpetually. At some point, decisions have to be made (for instances, translations have to be rendered, capitalization is either chosen or not, and so on), and these choices inevitably reflect the people making those decisions and judgments. On this score, the translators of the NRSV made a perfectly good translation when they rendered the instance of *ruach* in Genesis 1:2 as "wind," for they took into account the complexity of the word in its native context and made a viable judgment as a result. Perhaps this translation avoids some pitfalls and creates some generative possibilities amid the other possibilities available. But in this particular case, "God's spirit" is just as viable of a rendering, and with this choice, other potential ramifications can ensue—ones that do not necessarily follow from "a wind from God." On this last score, similarly to how the first chapter of the gospel of John picks up on the opening words of Genesis ("in the beginning") and reworks the notion of "word" given the act of God speaking, one could see a corollary move made in terms of a pneumatological construal in light of "God's spirit sweeping over the face of the waters." Theologically speaking, both the "word of God" and the "spirit of God" can be said to be operative in the creation account of Genesis 1. When such kinds of gestures are possible, Christians are well within hermeneutical propriety in pursuing them given that the OT is Christian Scripture.

The warrants for a perspectival duality

As one makes headway through the OT materials on Spirit-matters, one sees a number of possibilities that may not be as readily apparent in the NT. One such example is the OT's association of the

Spirit with life and creation. Not only is the point available in the depiction of God's *ruach* brooding or sweeping over the waters of the formless void but in other isolated instances as well.[5] Although not explicitly containing *ruach* language, some have also included the instance of God breathing life into the first humans (Gen 2:7) as a further indicator of this gesture of connecting the beginning and perpetuation of life with the Spirit of God. Although Genesis 2 is an outlier in this way, a number of passages do use *ruach* similarly.[6] Pivotal here is the testimony of the prophet Ezekiel: His vision of the "Valley of Dry Bones" is rich with life-giving Spirit-imagery. After the prophet is led by the Spirit of YHWH to the valley, he is told to prophesy to the bones therein, "Thus says the Lord God to these bones: I will cause *ruach* to enter you, and you shall live. I will lay sinews on you, and will cause flesh to come upon you, and cover you with skin, and you shall live; and you shall know that I am YHWH" (Ezek 37:5–6). Once the bodies were constituted yet lifeless, Ezekiel is further instructed: "Prophesy to the *ruach*, prophesy, mortal, and say to the *ruach*: Thus says the Lord God: Come from the four *ruachim*, o *ruach*, and breathe upon these slain, that they may live" (Ezek 37:9). Given the historical context of Ezekiel, the passage can be taken to be referring to the rebirth and restoration of Israel, but it also helps show how the Spirit is originary to life and vitality in a crucial way—be it "created" or "resurrected" life.

As this passage and others show, the connection between *ruach* and life is important. The connection underscores that God the Spirit is—to echo the Nicene-Constantinopolitan Creed—"the Lord and Giver of life." In a fundamental way, life would simply not be apart from the One who has given shape, meaning, and vitality to the formless void. In this sense, life is dependent on God's Spirit in a special way. One only need to look at the Genesis creation accounts in tandem to show the point in another way: Whereas in Genesis 1 what is distinct about the touchpoint between God and humans is that the latter are created in God's image, in Genesis 2 the distinct touchpoint involves God breathing into the first human. George

---

[5]A random sampling could include Job 26:13, Psalm 104:30, and Ecclesiastes 12:7.
[6]See Genesis 6:3, several passages in Job (27:3, 32:8, 33:4, and 34:14), and Isaiah 42:5 for some of these cases.

Montague expresses the connection compellingly: "Man's breath of life is a direct gift of God to him. It is not said of any other of God's creatures in this account that he gave them the breath of life in this way. He planted a garden (2:8), he made trees grow (2:9), he 'formed animals' of all kinds out of the ground (2:19), but it is never said that he breathed the breath of life into their nostrils. This suggests that man's life is a more intimate gift from the Lord than is that of the rest of creation."[7] Functionally, then, a relationship can be made between the "image/likeness" language of Genesis 1 and the breath of life being breathed into humanity's nostrils by God in Genesis 2.

At the same time, the act of giving life is ultimately one of hospitality, of making room and accommodating the existence of a distinct, identifiable other. When God gives life, something other than God comes to be. In this particular way of casting the matter, life is independent of God. At play here are concerns related to the doctrine of creation, a theme that will be treated more substantively in a subsequent chapter of this work. But for the moment, one can say that the Creator-creation interface creates a perspectival duality: One can think of God moving to creatures, or one can think of creatures—operating out of their grace-enabled capacity as God's creatures—as subsequently moving to God. The former, obviously, is always conceptually primordial ("before all else, God is"), yet the latter is more attuned to the way humans experience themselves and their reality as they begin the act of reflection already out of the contingencies of their creaturely constitution. To put the matter in the words of Dietrich Bonhoeffer, humans are always and already "in the middle" of creaturely constraints and possibilities.[8] In pneumatological terms, God's *ruach* is different from humanity's *ruach* because God and humans are different, yet a connection is also implied—and on the basis of this connection a singular term is permissible—on the ground that God is the beginning and end of all life, including human life.

[7]George T. Montague, *The Holy Spirit: The Growth of a Biblical Tradition* (Eugene, OR: Wipf and Stock, 2006), p. 6.
[8]Dietrich Bonhoeffer, *Creation and Fall: A Theological Exposition of Genesis 1–3*, trans. Douglas Stephen Bax (Minneapolis: Fortress Press, 1997), p. 28.

Pneumatology from below

The delineations above are important to maintain because one running feature of Spirit-talk in the OT is its earthiness or mundanity. This quality may be difficult for NT-shaped readers of the OT to appreciate. However, one cannot deny that Spirit-language makes its way in the OT not simply in extraordinary displays of God's presence and power but also in relation to important yet oftentimes deemed "this-worldly" realities and activities.[9] In order to recognize this strand of Spirit-speech in the Bible, one can speak of a "pneumatology from below."[10] What is meant by a "pneumatology from below" is the collective witness of those instances of Spirit-talk in the OT in which creatures exhibit, live in accordance, and flourish in terms of the *ruach* in them, which has its source and end in the *ruach* of God. This is an "earthy" depiction of spiritual realities, one that suggests emergence more so than rupture and continuity with what and who the creature is and is meant to be rather than discontinuity in terms of the limits or brokenness/ fallenness of humanity.

Although the pertinent examples within this category are not numerous, they are important to note. For instance, a series of passages within the Torah employs the term *ruach* in association with skill, wisdom, and craftsmanship.[11] Notable about many of these passages is that the *ruach* in question comes from God but

---

[9]One of the most important advocates for this perspective writing today would be John R. Levison. See his important work *Filled with the Spirit* (Grand Rapids, MI: Eerdmans, 2009).

[10]A number of constructs within systematic theology and biblical studies are framed typologically in terms of "from below" and "from above," and so it is quite natural to use these here. It should be noted that sometimes these typologies work on strong ideological lines, ones framed in terms of a strict "faith versus reason" or "revelation versus history" logic. Those resonances are not implied here. "From below" and "from above" in the present case point to a perspectival differentiation in terms of the Holy Spirit's one work of renewal and sanctification. In other words, at play is one work of God's Spirit understood from two vantage points. These could be framed in terms of "emergence" (in which the Spirit works within God-given capacities granted at the point of creation) and "rupture" (in which the Spirit prompts and enables capacities that are otherwise unexpected given how creation is typically understood). A third way of narrating the dynamic could be in terms of "excellence" and "surprise."

[11]See for instance Exodus 28:3, 31:3, 35:31; Numbers 27:18; and Deuteronomy 34:9, among others.

its manifestation often is in terms of mundane matters tied to the good of the community including the making of priestly vestments, devising artistic designs, and authority and wisdom for governance. At play in these would be the striving after, cultivation, and execution of human flourishing and excellence. One could also include at this juncture the practice of virtue and tending to the life of the mind.[12]

Take for instance Numbers 11. The spirit on Moses, which is later identified by Moses as YHWH's Spirit (Num 11:29), is distributed to the 70 elders as a way of helping Moses govern and lead the people of Israel in their desert sojourning. When Moses and the elders gathered together, YHWH "came down in the cloud and spoke to [Moses] and [YHWH] took some of the spirit that was on [Moses] and put it on the seventy elders; and when the spirit rested upon them, they prophesied" (Num 11:25). This example should prove positive to Christians because it ties Spirit-speech to something acceptable as orderly and proper governance. The Spirit is not just for a single, charismatic, specially endowed leader but for the many who are charged to help the people in their desert/faith peregrination. Therefore, this passage's depiction of the Spirit within "this-worldly" concerns involves the Spirit being shared and tied to the good of the community as a whole.

A more difficult depiction of the earthiness of *ruach* is the strength associated with the judge Samson. Early in his life, Samson was stirred by the Spirit of YHWH (Judg 13:25), but this stirring appears to work Samson into a kind of frenzy, one which grants him the strength and skill not only to destroy a lion barehanded (Judg 14:6) but also to kill 30 men at Ashkelon (Judg 14:19) and 1,000 Philistines with a jawbone of a donkey (Judg 15:14). Rather than helping Israel's leadership in self-governance, Spirit-fruition is depicted in this case as playing a role within Israelite nationalism through the vengeful acts by one of its judges upon Israel's enemies.[13] A number of questions naturally arise with this example for those of us removed from these circumstances and shaped by the sensibilities inherent to Jesus' teachings. But for a people caught up in a struggle for survival and taunted by surrounding

---

[12]See broader considerations of these themes in John R. Levison, *Inspired: The Holy Spirit and the Mind of Faith* (Grand Rapids, MI: Eerdmans, 2013).

[13]Although less controversial perhaps, Gideon—who was deftly able against the Midianites because of a kind of Spirit-possession (Judges 6:34)—would be a related example.

powerful forces, the prospect of the Spirit raising national heroes who are mighty and powerful would be compelling. This example shows another—if admittedly more challenging—example of the Spirit's "earthy" portrayals in the OT.

Pneumatology from above

As the previous references show, the Spirit works within earthy contingencies and particularities to help the faithful amid their everyday roles, responsibilities, and challenges. Typically, however, Christians normally think of the Spirit as coming or falling upon God-fearers so that they function charismatically and proclaim powerfully both God's judgment and salvation. This kind of phenomenon is a NT pattern to be sure, but it is also found in the OT, usually in terms of the prophetic office and various roles of preeminence. Plenty of examples of this kind can be identified. For example, Saul is worked up into a prophetic frenzy when the Spirit of God overtakes him around the time he is anointed king (see 1 Sam 10). Saul's inclusion into the prophetic ranks was unusual even for those who were eyewitnesses of these events (vv. 11–12) as well as for us today since usually people associate the prophetic role with tasks of warning the people of their wayward ways[14] as well as giving them hope for a brighter and more promising future if they heed the call to repentance. As for the judges, these are often depicted in the OT within a cycle that involves Israel's disobedience, God's judgment, repentance by the people, and the activity of a judge who brings about stability or victory for the people resulting in peace and prosperity—that is until the cycle repeats itself.[15] In the cases of both prophets and judges, God's Spirit plays a crucial role in raising and anointing them for their tasks. Because of their unusual and "other-worldly" activities, these examples collectively function to represent what could be considered a "pneumatology from above."

---

[14]See Nehemiah 9:30.
[15]For elaborations of this cycle, see Anthony C. Thiselton, *The Holy Spirit—In Biblical Teaching, through the Centuries, and Today* (Grand Rapids, MI: Eerdmans, 2013), pp. 10–11. As Thiselton notes, many of these judges have particular weaknesses that magnify the way their role is inhabitable and effective only by the mercy and activity of God's Spirit (p. 11).

Speech pertaining to a "pneumatology from above" is especially prominent in the canonical book of Isaiah in light of passages that typically have a messianic and so Christological relevance for Christians. For instance, Isaiah 11 speaks of a "shoot from the stump of Jesse" upon whom the Spirit of YHWH will rest, a Spirit of wisdom, understanding, and the like. Another case is Isaiah 40: This passage is typically associated with the preaching of John the Baptist, and within it are references to the Spirit of YHWH (verses 7 and 13). Isaiah 42—which is the first of the Servant Songs of Isaiah—depicts the Servant as having God's Spirit upon him as he brings forth justice to the nations (v. 1)[16] and teaches them. And finally, Isaiah 61 begins with the gospel passage which Jesus claims is fulfilled in his person:[17] "The Spirit of the Lord GOD is upon me, because the LORD has anointed me; he has sent me to bring good news to the oppressed, to bind up the brokenhearted, to proclaim liberty to the captives, and release to the prisoners." Within the Christian imaginary, these Isaiah passages help cultivate at least two related claims: Jesus' ministry can be seen as both prophetic and charismatic, and the pattern of the Spirit calling and anointing leaders is a running, cross-testamental theme within the Bible.

Conclusion

Old Testament Spirit-references are not easily categorized. We have offered the heuristic devices "from below" and "from above" in order to cast some meaning-generating order on the relevant material. It should be duly noted that this approach is "perspectival" in the sense of fostering different approaches to facilitate the appreciation of the collective whole. In no sense should the language be reified so as to pigeonhole individual cases into permanently sealed boxes. In other words, a passage deemed here or elsewhere as "from below" or "from above" should not be taken as irrefutably and permanently so; again, these are simply provisional measures. Nevertheless, the heritage of the OT witness is sufficiently rich and diverse so as to ground and inflect Christian pneumatology in a multitude of

---

[16]See Matthew 12:18.
[17]See Luke 4:18ff.

ways, and various strategies and categories should be employed to communicate this vastness.

Second Temple Judaism

Although most Christians know very little of the time period between the last canonical prophets and the beginnings of the Christian church, its influence is very much detectable in the early Christian literature. This recognition only makes sense: The expanse of time between the testaments is centuries wide, so the immediate context of the first Christians would be one that was indebted and influenced by its immediate environs in ways that canonical writings simply could not have been. Some of the importance of that period for the nascent Christian church was advocated by Hermann Gunkel.[18] In the estimation of John Levison, Gunkel was correct to emphasize the importance of Judaism for early Christian reflection on pneumatology but was wrong in his assessment or characterization of that influence.[19] For Gunkel, little Spirit-phenomena were available at this time, but Levison disagrees by believing this period to be rich with vitality on the theme. One suspects that part of Gunkel's assessment stems from prominent narratives that hailed the end of Jewish prophecy (which took place in the eyes of many with the deaths of the prophets Haggai, Zechariah, and Malachi) and in turn associated this development with the withdrawing of the Spirit from Judaism.[20] As popular as this narrative has been, one cannot help but recognize that the announced withdrawing of the Spirit was a claim unduly attendant to various, relevant strands.

As with OT materials, so in these cases: One can identify pneumatological emphases and patterns that can be understood as "from below" and "from above." Take for instance the work of Jesus Ben Sira sometimes referred to as "the Wisdom of Sirach,"

---

[18]See Hermann Gunkel, *The Influence of the Holy Spirit: The Popular View of the Apostolic Age and the Teachings of the Apostle Paul*, trans. Roy A. Harrisville and Philip A. Quanbeck II (Philadelphia, PA: Fortress Press, 1979).

[19]See Levison, *Filled with the Spirit*, p. 112.

[20]For a survey of readings in this vein, see Levison, *Filled with the Spirit*, pp. 115–16 as well as his "Did the Spirit Withdraw from Israel?" *New Testament Studies* 43 (1997): 35–57.

"Ecclesiasticus," or just simply "Sirach." As a founder of a scribal academy in Jerusalem, Ben Sira considered it important to emphasize study for its role in the cultivation of wisdom and inspiration. Mentorship is a crucial emphasis in this process, for people seeking wisdom ought to seek the council of the elders and to attach oneself to them so that their doorsteps are worn out (see 6:36). The role of dreams, something potentially attributable to a "from above" sensibility, is significantly downplayed by Ben Sira, for he believes dreams give wings to fools, they reflect those who have them, and ultimately they are impure and unreal (see 34:1–5). The alternative to these flights of fancy would be travel, study, experience, and fearing the Lord. The point is summarized in the following: "How different the one who devotes himself to the study of the law of the Most High! He seeks out the wisdom of all the ancients . . . he preserves the sayings of the famous . . . he serves among the great and appears before rulers . . . He sets his heart to rise early to seek the Lord who made him . . . If the great Lord is willing, he will be filled with the spirit of understanding."[21] The work of the Spirit in terms of inspiration and wisdom is very much tied here to human steadfastness, diligence, and learning.

Or in a similar "from below" vein, consider the addition to Daniel known as "Susanna," in which Daniel comes to the defense of the titular figure who is wrongly accused by vile elders. As Susanna raises a cry to God for help, the work proceeds to narrate: "The Lord heard her cry. Just as she was being led off to execution, God stirred up the holy spirit of a young lad named Daniel, and he shouted with a loud voice, 'I want no part in shedding this woman's blood!'" (vv. 44–46). What is particularly appealing about this account is that apparently Daniel's spirit, which was stirred for justice, was already holy. Piety and justice are thus not considered antithetical in this passage; they work hand in hand in a very important way. God's Holy Spirit[22] not only stirs people but God also stirs those who are already devoted to God, and this stirring is not simply for ecstatic fits of rapture but also to defend the righteous and innocent.

---

[21]Sirach 38:34–39:6.
[22]The reference to "*Holy* Spirit" is somewhat late in the canonical writings. Two texts from the OT (Psalm 51:11 and Isaiah 63:11) are usually cited, but the literature of the Second Temple period is also important for the theme (in addition to the passage above one can also find references in Wisdom 9:17, 2 Esdras 14:22, and a number of places in the Dead Sea Scrolls).

At the same time, one does find "from above" tendencies in the literature of this time period. One need only look to the "Wisdom of Solomon." Various Spirit-themes come to the fore in this work, but early on, the writer remarks, "Because the spirit of the Lord has filled the world, and that which holds all things together knows what is said, therefore those who utter unrighteous things will not escape notice, and justice, when it punishes, will not pass them by" (Wis 1:7–8). As a sapiential writing, the Wisdom of Solomon is concerned with matters such as deceit, righteousness, and so on; however, the work in particular offers a Spirit-perspective "from above," for what happens on earth is inflected, observed, and taken into account by the Spirit who has filled and holds this world together. To pick up on another theme associated with pneumatology, the writer mentions God as the source of life and not death (1:13–14; take note of 12:1 as well: "For your immortal spirit is in all things"). Later in the work, when Solomon is said to speak, he talks of his mortality and commonness with all other creatures, but he goes on to say, "Therefore I prayed, and understanding was given me; I called on God, and the spirit of wisdom came to me" (7:7). As the speaker personifies wisdom, he describes it in lofty and expanded ways: "There is in her a spirit that is intelligent, holy, unique, manifold, subtle, mobile, clear, unpolluted, distinct, invulnerable, loving the good, keen, irresistible, beneficent, humane, steadfast, sure, free from anxiety, all-powerful, overseeing all, and penetrating through all spirits that are intelligent, pure, and altogether subtle" (7:22–23). He furthermore remarks, "For she is a breath of the power of God, and a pure emanation of the glory of the Almighty; therefore nothing defiled gains entrance into her. For she is a reflection of eternal light, a spotless mirror of the working of God, and an image of his goodness. Although she is but one, she can do all things, and while remaining in herself, she renews all things; in every generation she passes into holy souls and makes them friends of God, and prophets" (7:25–27). When one couples these elaborations of Wisdom with the claim by some early Christians (particularly Irenaeus) that the Holy Spirit can be understood in terms of personified Wisdom, one generates a sense that the Holy Spirit comes and transforms those who actively seek, love, and enjoy God. As the speaker remarks later looking back at his life: "But I perceived that I would not possess wisdom unless God gave her to me—and it was a mark of insight to know whose gift she was—so I appealed to the Lord and implored him" (8:21), and later, "Who has learned your counsel, unless you have given wisdom and sent your holy spirit from on high?" (9:17).

The New Testament

In the NT, Spirit-talk is registered in terms of *pneuma*, which, as already noted in this work, is the rough equivalent to *ruach*. Therefore, *pneuma* can also refer to a person's spirit, evil spirits, and a general spirit-realm. At the same time, Spirit-speech in the NT is not as wide-ranging as the OT; it is picked up largely in terms of soteriology and exhibits degrees of greater determinateness. Many of the instances in the NT lend themselves to being categorized as exhibiting "from above" patterns. In other words, Spirit-instances in the NT typically do not appear as earthy as some of those found in the OT. Examples in the NT broadly, however, are vast, and once again, only a brief survey of some of the most prominent cases can be entertained in the following.

The Synoptic gospels

In terms of the first three gospels, the synoptics depict John the Baptist proclaiming that the One to come would baptize with or in the Holy Spirit (Matt 3:11; Mark 1:8; Luke 3:16), but chronologically before his preaching, Jesus is said to be conceived through the activity of the Holy Spirit by both Matthew (1:18, 20) and Luke (1:35).[23] Particularly striking is the way Spirit-speech permeates the first chapters of Luke, for Spirit-talk is associated with prophecies related to John the Baptist's life (1:15), his pregnant mother Elizabeth (1:41), his father Zechariah upon his ability to speak once more (1:67), and Simeon of Jerusalem (2:25–26). At Jesus' baptism by John, the Spirit descended upon Jesus in the

---

[23]With these cases, I do not wish to entangle myself further in the complication of articular definition in Spirit-talk. That these cases do not have the definite article in the textual evidence may simply be a matter of grammatical concern (i.e. they are anarthrous), which is an approach taken by many scholars. The theological purchase of this phenomenon is unclear and proposals to explain it are speculative.

form of a dove (Luke 3:22) and Jesus was filled (Luke 4:1) and led (Matt 4:1) or driven (Mark 1:12) by the Spirit into the desert to be tempted by the devil.

After these initial remarks, these gospels vary in terms of their Spirit-speech. For Matthew and Mark, reference is made to blasphemy against the Holy Spirit,[24] David speaking by the Holy Spirit in what is an OT allusion,[25] and the disciples being told they will be conduits for the Spirit's speech when they are put on trial.[26] But as noted above, Luke demonstrates more numerous cases of such language. On several occasions, Luke presents Jesus as a charismatic figure who is filled with the Spirit and who speaks with authority and works in power.[27] Luke has Jesus rejoicing in the Spirit (10:21) and mentions that the Spirit will be given to those who ask (11:13).

The Johannine literature

The NT writings associated with John have distinct pneumatological emphases, pericopes, and themes. In terms of the gospel of John, the event of Jesus' baptism is also pneumatologically depicted but in its own way. Also unique is the interchange between Jesus and Nicodemus in which Jesus remarks of the need to be "born of the Spirit" (John 3:6, 8). As the one who gives the "Spirit without measure" (3:34), Jesus also remarks of the need to worship the Father in "spirit and truth" (4:23–24). In addition to truth, John also depicts the Spirit with life (6:63), yet this claim stands in tension with a remark made in Chapter 7: "Now [Jesus] said this about the Spirit, which believers in him were to receive; for as yet there was no Spirit, because Jesus was not yet glorified" (v. 39). This last foreshadowed instance comes to fruition when after the resurrection Jesus breaths on his disciples and tells them, "Receive the Holy Spirit" (20:22). In this sense, for John, "The Spirit . . . is given to the community through the glorification of Jesus in his passion."[28] This gesture toward the passion is at play most prominently in the

---

[24]Matthew 12:31 and Mark 3:29; a similar reference is also found in Luke 12:10.
[25]Matthew 22:43 and Mark 12:36.
[26]Matthew 10:20 and Mark 13:11. See also Luke 12:12.
[27]For just a small sampling, see Luke 5:17 and 6:19.
[28]Gary D. Badcock, *Light of Truth and Fire of Love: A Theology of the Holy Spirit* (Grand Rapids, MI: Eerdmans, 1997), p. 28.

"Farewell Discourses" of John 14–17, a section of material that has and will continue to be of great importance in this book.

The remaining instances of Spirit-talk within the Johannine literature are sporadic allusions. First John shares themes with John's gospel by identifying the Spirit as being given by Jesus (1 John 3:24). This link between the Spirit and Jesus is further extended in terms of discernment: John remarks that the spirits need to be tested, and one knows the Spirit of God because "every spirit that confesses that Jesus Christ has come in the flesh is from God" (4:2). Retaining the "abiding/remaining" language of the Farewell Discourses, First John further adds that disciples can know of this Spirit-disciple interpenetration because Jesus has given his Spirit (4:13). As such, the Spirit testifies and the Spirit is truth (see 5:6). As for the Book of Revelation, in multiple instances the Seer is confirmed as "in the Spirit" (Rev 4:2, 17:3, 21:10), and his prophecies to the Seven Churches are each concluded with the refrain that anyone who has an ear should listen to what the Spirit is saying to the churches (2:7, 11, 17, 29; 3:6, 13, 22). In addition to reference to the "seven spirits" (4:5, 6:7), the Seer mentions the Spirit of prophecy (19:10), the spirits of prophets (22:6), and the Spirit of life (11:11). Finally, the Spirit speaks solely (14:13) and alongside the bride (22:17).

Acts

In addition to his gospel, Luke is associated with the book called "Acts" or *praxeis*. Given Luke's themes in his gospel as well as in this text, one could make the case that the "acts" in question are of the Holy Spirit *and* the apostles since an ongoing synergy between the two is apparent in this book. This interconnectivity is foreshadowed when the apostles are instructed to wait in Jerusalem for the "promise of the Father" in fulfillment of John the Baptist's preaching, a baptism not of water but by and with the Holy Spirit. According to Jesus, they would receive power from the Spirit at that time to be witnesses throughout the world (1:8).

Acts makes a point to draw connections between the OT and the Spirit-developments it documents. Luke emphasizes that Judas' betrayal was foretold by David via the Spirit as he goes on to speak of how the early church went about choosing a replacement for Judas (1:16). Luke claimed David to be an "in-spirited" figure one other time (see 4:25) and claims the same to be the case for the prophet Isaiah (28:25). But one of the most prominent instances of Spirit-talk in Acts is the quotation of Joel's prophecy in Peter's Sermon on the Day of Pentecost. Peter recalls what Joel said (cf. Joel 2:28–29) in order to make sense of those who at the moment were speaking in other languages as a result of the Spirit's filling (2:4): "In the last days it will be, God declares, that I will pour out my Spirit upon all flesh, and your sons and your daughters shall prophesy, and your young men shall see visions, and your old men shall dream dreams. Even upon my slaves, both men and women, in those days I will pour out my Spirit; and they shall prophesy" (2:17–18). Tying Jesus into this vision as its fulfillment, Peter concludes, "This Jesus God raised up, and of that all of us are witnesses. Being therefore exalted at the right hand of God, and having received from the Father the promise of the Holy Spirit, he has poured out this that you both see and hear" (2:32–33).

Acts also depicts many instances of the Spirit filling or falling upon people as a gift that empowers their witness and mission. In addition to the Day of Pentecost occurrence, instances of this kind include Peter's connection of baptism with this filling (2:38), the case of Peter himself (4:8), the believers who were gathered to receive Peter and John upon their release from prison (4:31), the promise that this reception would take place upon those who obey God (5:32), the ministry of Peter and John in Samaria (8:14–17), Saul/Paul (9:17; also 13:9), Cornelius' house (10:44–45; see also 15:8), the disciples at Antioch (13:52), and the assumed logic of Paul through his questioning of the Ephesians (19:1–7). Stephen is also repeatedly mentioned as one full or filled with the Spirit and the Spirit's wisdom (6:5, 10; 7:55).

In Stephen's speech to his eventual executioners, he makes a remark that continually applies to the synergistic interplay one sees in Acts; in the words of the first Christian martyr: "You stiff-necked people, uncircumcised in heart and ears, you are forever opposing the Holy Spirit, just as your ancestors used to do" (7:51). These remarks affirm the continual work of the Spirit in and among a people who in turn work against this activity. The same kind of synergistic logic is implied earlier in the case of Ananias and Sapphira, who lied (5:3) and put the Spirit to the test (5:9), respectively. These examples show that amid the widespread reported acts of the Spirit, humans could work alongside or against such activity in their own, proper acts. This theme of synergy or cooperation is echoed elsewhere in the NT.[29]

Pauline epistles

When considering the Pauline corpus, one notes a number of important characteristics in Spirit-talk. Although not necessarily unique to Paul, one does notice the way the Apostle often associates the Spirit with a kind of renewing or formative role. This point is made in reference to the Son (Rom 1:4) as well as to Paul's own ministry[30] and in relation to his hearers.[31] Second, Paul makes mention of the Spirit as One who comes to believers in a distinct act, which is in keeping with what we have noted about a "pneumatology from above." The Spirit is given as a first installment (2 Cor 1:22; see also 5:5 and Eph 1:14)[32] and received by the disciples (Gal 3:2). Third, the Spirit is the medium of God's love (Rom 5:5; 15:30) and so is at work in one's transformation (2 Cor 3:3) and sanctification (Rom 15:16; see also 1 Cor 6:11 and 2 Thes 2:13). In this sense, the Spirit is the Spirit of the Son (Gal 4:6; see also Rom 8:9 and Phil 1:19): Whoever confesses Jesus does so in the Spirit (1 Cor 12:3), for one is born (Gal 4:29) and justified by the Spirit (1 Cor 6:11; see also 2 Cor 3:8–9 and Gal 5:5). The Spirit is the author of life and is in fact Lord (2 Cor 3:6, 17). In worshiping by the Spirit (Phil 3:3), the church receives a number of gifts (1 Cor 12) and fruits (Gal 5:22–23) so that believers may be "heirs according to the hope of eternal life" (Titus 3:7). With these many references, one can see the rationale for Gordon Fee's claim: "For Paul the Spirit, as an experienced and living reality, was the absolutely crucial matter for Christian life, from beginning to end."[33]

---

[29]Other relevant passages would include Matthew 12:31–32, Acts 7:51, Ephesians 4:30, 1 Thessalonians 5:19–21, and Hebrews 10:26–29.

[30]Romans 15:19, 1 Corinthians 2:4, and 1 Thessalonians 1:5.

[31]Romans 15:13 and 2 Timothy 1:7.

[32]This metaphor (which could also be translated as "down payment") as well as "first fruits" (Rom 8:23) and "seal" (2 Cor 1:21–22; Eph 1:13, 4:30) demonstrate the eschatological character of Paul's pneumatology; see Gordon D. Fee, *God's Empowering Presence* (Peabody, MA: Hendrickson, 1994), chapter 12.

[33]Fee, *God's Empowering Presence*, p. 1.

One extensive Pauline passage that illustrates this last point is Romans 8. Paul describes here what he alludes to earlier as leading "the new life of the Spirit" (Rom 7:6). This life involves the claim that the law of the Spirit sets believers free (8:2) so that they no longer have to walk according to the flesh but according to the Spirit (v. 4). Having the mind of the Spirit means life and peace (v. 6). This One dwells in followers of Jesus; it is because of the Spirit that they belong to Christ, for the One who raised Jesus gives disciples hope that they are children of God. This Spirit bears witness with the human spirit that disciples are joint heirs with Christ. As such the Spirit helps believers in their weakness "with sighs too deep for words" (v. 26).[34] This One's intercession is according to the will of God and is the background to the claim that "all things work together for good for those who love God" (v. 28).

Sporadic references to the Spirit are also made in other works. In Ephesians, the Spirit is associated with Christian unity.[35] Christians are called to be of "one spirit" (2:18), for division "grieves the Spirit" (4:30). As such, the Ephesians are to be filled with the Spirit (5:18) as they engage in the sundry work of the church. Finally, the Pastoral Epistles make some references to the Spirit. The mystery of faith is alluded to in terms of the Spirit vindicating Christ (1 Tim 3:16), and one can also find the inspiration of Scripture passage in 2 Timothy 3:16, with the key term having a form of *pneuma* at its root ("God-breathed"). Important to note is Titus 3, which identifies the Spirit's role the following way: "This Spirit he poured out on us richly through Jesus Christ our Savior, so that, having been justified by his grace, we might become heirs according to the hope of eternal life" (vv. 6–7). This passage can be deemed as the "quintessential summary of Pauline pneumatology" not only in the Pastorals but perhaps even in the whole of the Pauline corpus.[36]

---

[34]See also Philippians 1:19 and 2 Timothy 1:14.

[35]This same point is sounded in Jude 19: "It is these worldly people, devoid of the Spirit, who are causing divisions." Jude's hearers are encouraged to do otherwise, including to "pray in the Holy Spirit" (v. 20).

[36]Robert W. Wall, *1 & 2 Timothy and Titus* (Grand Rapids, MI: Eerdmans, 2012), p. 362.

Remaining New Testament letters

Many of the themes one finds in the remaining NT letters sound ideas already considered in this brief survey. The Letter to the Hebrews makes mention of the Spirit's gifts distributed according to God's will (2:4), references to the Spirit speaking in the OT are made (3:7, 10:15), an allusion is sustained that the Christian life involves a sharing in the Holy Spirit (6:4), and finally, Christ is said to offer himself through the Spirit as a sacrifice (9:14). The Petrine letters also make mention of the Spirit speaking through the prophets (1 Pet 1:11; 2 Pet 1:21), the Spirit's work of sanctification (1 Pet 1:2), the Spirit as the source of the gospel (1 Pet 1:12), the Spirit as the ground of Christ's resurrection (1 Pet 3:18), and the life of discipleship as pneumatically understood (1 Pet 4:6, 14).

The particular and underdetermined nature of biblical Spirit-talk

This survey of the biblical materials along the lines of Spirit-talk was necessarily brief and did not account for every relevant passage. However, distinct patterns across the Testaments are detectable. The Spirit anoints and commissions people to proclaim God's word and to do God's work in powerful and fruitful ways. The work of the Spirit goes by any number of terms, but sanctification and renewal are prominent themes. Scripture emphasizes that the Spirit was present and at work across the two Testaments, yet the theme of the Spirit coming in a distinct way among the disciples is also championed in the New. People can work alongside or against the Spirit in relation to activities that are both "earthy" (such as craftsmanship and governance) and "ordained" (prophetic frenzies and various kinds of charismatic speech, including tongues). Furthermore, the Spirit binds disciples in unity and purpose, which is telling since the Holy Spirit is the Spirit of Christ and the church is the body of Christ. An important interplay, then, is at hand among Christ, the Spirit, and the church.

Despite these many running themes and continuities, one should also notice the important ways Spirit-speech is continually ambiguous in the scriptural testimony. Issues of translation and capitalization, the relationship between a human spirit and God's Spirit, and the existence of a spirit-realm have already been mentioned in this book, but further specification in other matters is also pressing. For instance, if sanctification is a work of the Spirit, how is that work to be understood? What is the nature of prophecy and its role today, if any? How does one go about identifying spiritual gifts in the present? If Scripture is inspired, what does that claim mean, not simply theologically but epistemically and practically? As one can readily see, many of these matters are of vital importance to the Christian life, and various church traditions have answered them differently. Therefore, for all the many pneumatologically relevant passages in Scripture, plenty of contention and disagreement abound in today's contemporary climate on matters of pneumatological concern.

As this book will show to some degree, the history of Christian reflection on the Spirit yields a number of proposals and considerations that work together to drive the shape of pneumatology. Scripture provides tags, codings, patterns, and running themes that are exceptionally important, but subsequently different voices, figures, and traditions have gone on to employ these in support of varying—and sometimes contradicting—proposals. Therefore in terms of pneumatology, the Scriptural testimony provides a basic collage of concerns and themes that gain a certain life in the way they are appropriated. It is to the first stages of this process that we now turn.

3

The testimony of the Spirit

Pneumatology in the first centuries

*"When the Advocate comes, whom I will send to you
from the Father,
the Spirit of truth who comes from the Father,
[this One] will testify on my behalf.
You also are to testify because you have been with me from
the beginning"*

JOHN 15:26–27

In this book the case has been made repeatedly that Spirit-talk can be difficult to assess and appreciate because of its inherent ambiguity and indeterminacy. The biblical testimony, from which the shape and thrust of dogmatics extend, demonstrates these qualities in its Spirit-forms. For these and other reasons, pneumatology took some time to develop a modicum of enduring stability in Christian consciousness, and it has continued to grow and adapt in important ways. Regularly, when scholars and others wish to gain a historical and theological foothold within pneumatology, they focus on the fourth century and its ecumenical councils: Nicaea (325) and Constantinople (381). Nevertheless, developments and themes occurred before and after these major events. In what follows, then, some important voices and themes will be surveyed for the purpose of showing some of the qualities and issues associated with the earliest forms of Christian reflection on the Holy Spirit.

Pneumatology prior to Nicaea

Of course, pneumatological reflection was taking place prior to the fourth century, but it was typically affirmed in happenstance and occasional ways by early church leaders and thinkers of this era. As noted earlier, such tendencies follow the dominant pneumatological patterns of Scripture. Take for instance the collection of writings known as the witness of the "Apostolic Fathers."[1] In some of these writings, little to no mention of the Holy Spirit is made; in others, paltry few allusions can be found, and these usually are in passing, largely underdeveloped, and sometimes exceedingly unclear. Other writings in this collection are more noteworthy. For instance, in the letters of Ignatius of Antioch, the early church leader makes a visual reference to the Trinity in terms of proper teaching,[2] suggests that the conception of Christ is "from the seed of David and of the Holy Spirit,"[3] speaks of the prophets as Christ's disciples "in the Spirit,"[4] and mentions the Spirit countering deception by speaking through the apostolic preaching.[5] *The Didache*, an early Christian manual for teaching and practice that is also part of this collection, instructs believers to baptize according to the triune formula.[6] Furthermore, *The Shepherd of Hermas*, one of the most complex documents of this collection in that it displays both apocalyptic and allegorical qualities, speaks repeatedly of grieving the Holy Spirit in terms of "double-mindedness" and an angry temper.[7] The writing in this

---

[1]References to this collection will be to section and page numbers associated with the following edition and translation: Michael W. Holmes, *The Apostolic Fathers in English*, 3rd edition (Grand Rapids, MI: Baker Academic, 2006).
[2]*Letter to the Ephesians* 9.1 (p. 99).
[3]*Letter to the Ephesians* 18.2 (p. 101).
[4]*Letter to the Magnesians* 9.2 (p. 105).
[5]*Letter to the Philadelphians* 7 (p. 119).
[6]*The Didache*, 7 (p. 166).
[7]*The Shepherd of Hermas*, 41 (p. 236).

collection that is most explicitly pneumatological is the letter from the church at Rome to the church at Corinth known as *First Clement*. In this epistle, many references are made of the Spirit speaking in the OT in addition to the explicit citation of the "Holy Spirit" passage of Psalm 51. The letter's author pursues this course without the apparent worry of anachronism since the operative belief is that the Holy Spirit has given the Holy Scriptures, both Old and New Testaments, to the church.[8] This practice of recognizing the Holy Spirit in the OT was common by theologians throughout the time period.

Pneumatological development experienced a significant turn with the rise of a group of writers following the Apostolic Fathers. This group, some of whom are deemed the "Apologists," took on the task of defending the Christian faith to the broader culture in terms it could understand by showing Christianity's intellectual credibility as a path toward wisdom and virtue. This move was important since Christians were becoming more established within the wider customs, norms, and intellectual climates of their day. Yet during this period—roughly the second and third centuries— pneumatological reflection continued to be inchoate. Also at this time there emerged important rival groups within Christianity, ones that only increased the pressure for the church to stabilize and so institutionalize its beliefs, forms of organization, and ministries. Some of these were deemed to be on the fringes of Christian identity while others were actively resisted and eventually identified as heretical. In terms of pneumatology, some groups had little to no explicit concern to cite or mention the Spirit; the prime example here would be Marcionism. In contrast, other groups were marginalized or at odds with the dominant forms of Christianity precisely because of their Spirit-related beliefs and practices. This characterization is especially the case with Montanism or the "New Prophecy," which was founded by a leader who thought of himself and his community as benefitting and operating out of a special work of the Spirit. The Apologists, then, were not simply involved in defending Christianity to its "cultured despisers," although this feature of their work was important; they were also helping shape a subsequent generation of Christians by solidifying and maintaining the integrity of the teaching and traditions they had received. As

---

[8] *First Clement*, 45.2 (p. 63).

such, they were involved in the ongoing formulation of orthodoxy and refutation of heresy. Given some of the tensions at play during this period—including the ever-evolving doctrine of God, the nature of the Christian life and its spiritual marks and gifts, and the dynamic between charisma and institution in early church order—pneumatology became increasingly important.

In particular, the Spirit's identity and work gradually became explicit points of consideration. In terms of identity, the Spirit continually was referenced in formulaic patterns alongside the Father and Son. The Spirit was also repeatedly mentioned as working in ages past, a move that allowed for a degree of continuity in the economic outworking of God, particularly in terms of extending across the Testaments. Similarly to the case of Christ, the way Christians were speaking of the Spirit at this time rendered mounting pressure upon believers to think of the Spirit as more than simply a creature or an instrument of God. The Spirit was especially referenced in sacramental and other doxological activity, including Christian initiation and divinization.

Many figures belong to a discussion of Christian pneumatology prior to the fourth century, and unfortunately, given the constraints and scope of this book, an exhaustive treatment of the possibilities cannot be rendered. But by way of granting some form and substance to the present discussion, what follows will be surveys of three major leaders from this time period: Irenaeus (c.130–c.200), Tertullian (c.160–c.225), and Origen (c.185–c.254).

Irenaeus was Bishop of Lyons in southern Gaul, and he is known today via his works *Against Heresies* and *On the Apostolic Preaching*. The previous work is especially significant since in it Irenaeus identifies and opposes a number of heretical movements, primarily forms of Gnosticism but also Marcionism and Montanism. In his work, Irenaeus follows previous pneumatological patterns by mentioning the Spirit working through David and the prophets of the OT and invoking triune formulas and expressions. However, he goes one step further by speaking of the Christian faith in terms of "three articles" stratified along the lines of the Father (the Creator), Son (the Recapitulator and Mediator), and Holy Spirit, the latter being One "through whom the prophets prophesied and the patriarchs learnt the things of God and the righteous were led in the path of righteousness, and who, in the last times, was poured out in a new fashion upon the human race renewing man, throughout the world, to God."[9] Early on, Irenaeus was rendering the apostolic teaching or "rule of faith"[10] in a way which would be carried on in the structuring of the earliest creeds. Additionally, Irenaeus is famous for equating the Spirit with Wisdom[11] and in turn speaking of the Word and Wisdom as God's active "hands" within the economy of both creation and salvation.[12] The following quote shows the logic of this presentation of the "economic Trinity": "Thus, the Spirit demonstrates the Word, and, because of this, the prophets announced the Son of God, while the Word articulates the Spirit, and therefore it is He Himself who interprets the prophets and brings man to the Father."[13] In this sense, all three—Father, Son, and Holy Spirit—are involved in humans knowing and being transformed by God.[14] For Irenaeus, believers are baptized in the Spirit, continually indwelt and empowered by the Spirit, and will be raised from death by the Spirit.[15] From these points, one can conclude that the pneumatological continuity of God's work is crucial for Irenaeus.[16] Salvation is written in people's hearts by the Spirit and preserved by the ancient traditions.[17] It is in this sense of a traditioned community that one can understand another important pneumatological passage from Irenaeus:

[9]*On the Apostolic Preaching*, 6 as found in St. Irenaeus of Lyons, *On the Apostolic Preaching*, trans. John Behr (Crestwood, NY: St. Vladimir's Seminary Press, 1997), p. 44. This trifurcation is not original to Irenaeus but significantly exemplified by him. Most likely, the pattern has its origins in early baptismal questions and formulations.

[10]For some of Irenaeus' summaries of this "rule," see *Against Heresies*, 1.10.1 (*ANF*, 1:330–331) as well as 3.4.2 (p. 417).

[11]Irenaeus and Theophilus go against the tide of how both Scripture and tradition had generally been received in their day by opting to tie the Spirit—and not the Son—to Wisdom; for an extensive treatment of the topic, see Anthony Briggman, *Irenaeus of Lyons and the Theology of the Holy Spirit* (Oxford: Oxford University Press, 2012).

[12]Relevant passages include *Against Heresies*, 1.22.1 (*ANF*, 1:347), the Preface to Book 4 and its allusion to Gen 1:26 (p. 463), 4.20.1 (p. 487), and 5.6.1 (p. 531).

[13]*On the Apostolic Preaching*, 5 (p. 43).

[14]See *On the Apostolic Preaching*, 7 (p. 44) in which Irenaeus remarks, "the baptism of our regeneration takes place through these three articles, granting us regeneration unto God the Father through His Son by the Holy Spirit."

[15]See *On the Apostolic Preaching*, 41–42 (pp. 66–7).

[16]See *Against Heresies*, 3.1–2 (*ANF*, 1:414–415).

[17]*Against Heresies*, 3.4.2 (*ANF*, 1:417).

"Where the church is, there is the Spirit of God; and where the Spirit of God is, there is the church and every kind of grace."[18] As such, Christians are called to be Spirit-filled people, to walk in the light, and to tend toward perfection[19] as they stay true to what they have received.

Another figure worth mentioning at this point is Tertullian. Deemed by many as the father of Latin Christianity, Tertullian has often been cautiously received because of his association late in life with the aforementioned movement of Montanism, which was quite rigorous in its communal practices and held with suspicion by the Christian religious establishment. Nevertheless, he registered the Latin words "*trinitas*," "*persona*," and "*substantia*" for Christian God–grammar so that in his writings God is "Trinity" as "one substance, three persons." He made use of these terms primarily in his polemical work against a certain Praxeas (who, not incidentally, is identified by Tertullian as swaying the opinion of Rome against Montanism). Notice Tertullian's early usage of what would become key Trinitarian claims: "The mystery of the dispensation is still guarded which distributes the Unity into a Trinity placing in their order the three *Persons*—three, however, not in condition, but in degree; not in substance, but in form; not in power, but in aspect; yet of one substance, and of one condition, and of one power, inasmuch as He is one God, from whom these degrees and forms and aspects are reckoned, under the name of the Father, and of the Son, and of the Holy Ghost."[20] As such, the Spirit proceeds "from no other source than from the Father through the Son."[21] Tertullian further proves his prescience by anticipating future Trinitarian developments when he says that the Father, Son, and Spirit are inseparable from one another and that their enumeration is in terms of distinction or differentiation as opposed to division.[22] These claims helped shore both the divinity and individuation of the Holy Spirit, notions that would take years to be solidified in the consciousness of the broader church yet highlighted by this African leader quite early in the history of Christian reflection.

---

[18]*Against Heresies*, 3.24.1 (*ANF*, 1:458).
[19]*Against Heresies*, 5.8 (*ANF*, 1:533).
[20]*Against Praxeas*, 2 (*ANF*, 3:598).
[21]*Against Praxeas*, 4 (*ANF*, 3:599).
[22]See *Against Praxeas*, 9 (*ANF*, 3:603–604), 11 (pp. 605–6), and 12 (pp. 606–7); also note 25 (p. 621).

Of the contributions Tertullian makes to pneumatology,[23] this Trinitarian framing has proven especially helpful.

The final figure we will consider prior to the fourth century is Origen of Alexandria. Origen has been described as one of the greatest Christian thinkers of all time particularly because of the range and allegorical quality of his scriptural exegesis, although he has also been recognized for his important theological endeavoring through other kinds of productions, which would include the sometimes deemed "systematics" known as On First Principles. Origen is a very complex figure, and his reputation and reception in the church have been considerably mixed. This complexity is detectable in his Christological and pneumatological musings. Whereas he affirmed the eternal generation of the Son from the Father (so that "there was never a time when he was not"—a significant phrasing given what would develop with the Arian challenge), the latter nevertheless retained some kind of primordial status in being "Unbegotten." The same logic seems to hold in his pneumatology: The Spirit is apparently for Origen an eternal hypostasis as is the Father and the Son, yet the Father's status is such that this identity marks an important distinction within the triune life. This tension between these two streams is, according to Justo González, a mark of ante-Nicene Trinitarianism in that an unresolved contrast is typically promoted during this time period in terms of an "absolutely transcendent God" on the one hand and a "personal God of a limited transcendence who can therefore relate with creatures and establish dialogue with humans" on the other.[24] For these reasons, Origen can be said to have anticipated the Eastern conception of the Father as the "fount" or arche of divinity in God's mysterious, internal triune life, whereas others have seen Origen advocating a particular (and potentially problematic) form of subordinationism.[25] Origen made

---

[23]Tertullian also spoke repeatedly of the Spirit's role in prompting spiritual gifts (see, for instance, Against Marcion, 5.8 [ANF, 3:446]) and in maturing and perfecting believers (see, for example, On the Veiling of Virgins, 1 [ANF, 4:27]); he also maintains that Spirit-baptism is something different from water baptism (see On Baptism, 6 [ANF, 3:672] and 10 [p. 674]).

[24]Justo L. González, A History of Christian Thought, vol. 1, rev. ed. (Nashville, TN: Abingdon, 1987), pp. 218–19.

[25]The term "subordinationism" may be misleading in Origen's case; perhaps "dependence" would be better. See Lewis Ayres, Nicaea and Its Legacy: An Approach to Fourth-Century Trinitarian Theology (Oxford: Oxford University Press, 2004), p. 23.

some other important claims about the Spirit, including drawing
the connection between the OT "Spirit of God" and the NT "Holy
Spirit" on spiritual (and explicitly non-historical) grounds[26] as well
as making the point that salvation/divinization is necessarily a work
of the entire Trinity.[27] Finally, he emphasizes repeatedly the distinct
work of the Spirit in the sanctification of believers.[28]

The fourth century

Despite these early reflections on the Spirit, theological controversies
and attention were directed primarily to issues related to the Son prior
to Nicaea. This focus is understandable in that the Christian doctrine
of God up to this point had largely been debated in binitarian terms,
that is, marked by reference to the Son and Father. The mounting
pressure at this stage surrounded the question of whether the Son
was truly God. Only after this matter had received considerable
attention did the question of the Spirit's divinity receive its due
consideration. When the Council of Nicaea finished its deliberations,
the resulting creed reflected its context and orienting concerns: The
tripartite pattern (as noted above) was maintained, but the most
elaborate clause or article was on the Son. The Nicene Creed at this
time in/famously affirmed belief "in the Holy Spirit" with nothing
else by way of substantiation. The glaring brevity of expression
simply beckoned for more in the following years, and more did in
fact materialize because of varied and contested alternatives that
were brought to the fore. Therefore what took place in the rest of
the fourth century was not only an ongoing struggle to clarify and
secure Nicene orthodoxy but also efforts toward pneumatological
substantiation that in turn contributed to the further refinement of
Christian Trinitarianism. A culminating moment in this process was
Constantinople's more elaborate expression of the Third Article:
"We believe . . . in the Holy Spirit, the Lord and the Life-Giver,

---

[26]*On First Principles*, 1.3.3 (*ANF*, 4:252).
[27]*On First Principles*, 1.3.5 (*ANF*, 4:253). This is a controversial point: Origen
believed that the Spirit was only at work among believers.
[28]See for instance *On First Principles*, 1.3.8 (*ANF*, 4:255).

who proceeds from the Father, who is worshiped and glorified with the Father and the Son, who spoke through the prophets." As this formulation suggests, the church eventually settled on the claim that the Spirit is God of God.

Athanasius and the letters to Serapion

When one ventures to summarize pneumatological developments in the inter-conciliar period of the fourth century, Athanasius of Alexandria stands out as worthily considerable. Athanasius (c. 296–373) was present at Nicaea as part of his bishop's delegation, but he did not take an active role in the Council's proceedings. His profile became much more pronounced in the years that followed, for he gained the reputation of being "against the world" by maintaining his pro-Nicene stance in a variety of challenging and difficult circumstances, ones that repeatedly led to his exile.[29] Athanasius is remembered for a number of works, including *On the Incarnation*. This particular writing continues to be influential today in that it offers a compelling case for the divinity of the Son on the basis of soteriological propriety: The One who saves need be God, for this work could only be undertaken by the same One who brought the cosmos to be in the beginning. In other words, creation and salvation are integrally tied in that God, and only God, could undertake and enact both.[30]

Athanasius extended similar features of this Christological logic to the Spirit. In his *Letters to Serapion*, Athanasius counters those whom he deems "*Tropikoi*."[31] These figures considered the Spirit in what can be deemed an Arian way, thinking that the Spirit was a creature and a first-rate angel, and so less than fully God. Athanasius would have nothing to do with this framing, either in its Christological

---

[29]His political machinations have been recently brought to the fore, thereby affecting his contemporary reception; see the summary in R. P. C. Hanson, *The Search for the Christian Doctrine of God* (Edinburgh: T & T Clark, 1988), pp. 239–49.

[30]See *On the Incarnation*, 1 as found in St. Athanasius, *On the Incarnation*, trans. A Religious of C. S. M. V. (Crestwood, NY: St. Vladimir's Seminary Press, 2002), p. 26.

[31]This term relates to how these individuals interpreted "tropes" or metaphors in their scriptural exegesis. The numbering and translation used for Athanasius' *Letters to Serapion* will be from *Works on the Spirit: Athanasius the Great and Didymus the Blind*, trans. Mark DelCogliano, Andrew Radde-Gallwitz, and Lewis Ayres (Yonkers, St. Vladimir's Seminary Press, 2011).

or pneumatological forms. In the *Letters*, Athanasius argues that the work of the Spirit within the economy necessitates the Spirit's identification with divinity. The Spirit is the One who sanctifies and renews,[32] the One who gives rather than receives life,[33] and the One through whom humans are made partakers of God. In terms of the last point's relation to the divinity of the Spirit, Athanasius remarks, "But if we become sharers of the divine nature (cf. 2 Peter 1:4) by partaking of the Spirit, someone would have to be insane to say that the Spirit has a created nature and not the nature of God. For it is because of this that those in whom the Spirit dwells are divinized. And if he divinizes, there can be no doubt that his nature is of God."[34] In a move that would anticipate subsequent developments, he connects the *homoousios*—the term used at Nicaea to claim the Son as of the "same essence" as the Father—to the Spirit.[35] The logic that holds for claiming Christ's divinity is now similarly extended to the Spirit in these writings of Athanasius. His overall posture was confirmed through synodical deliberations at Alexandria in 362 where a variety of "Spirit-fighters" were denounced.[36]

The Cappadocians

Commentators have long-critiqued Athanasius for his lack of terminological rigor within Trinitarian reflection, particularly the uses he often made of the term *hypostasis*. Such efforts were undertaken by the group of theologians collectively known since the mid-nineteenth century as "the Cappadocians" because of their association with an ancient region in present-day Turkey and the many theological parallels that exist among these mutual acquaintances. They were Basil of Caesarea (c.330–c.370), his brother Gregory of Nyssa (c.335–c.394), and their friend Gregory of Nazianzus (c.329–c.390). Among their achievements, they were

---

[32]*Letters to Serapion*, 1.22.3 (p. 88).
[33]*Letters to Serapion*, 1.23.2 (p. 89).
[34]*Letters to Serapion*, 1.24.4 (p. 90).
[35]*Letters to Serapion*, 1.27.3 (p. 96).
[36]Sometimes these opponents of the Spirit are called "Macedonians," which is a misleading name. For a summary of their views, see Hanson, *The Search for the Christian Doctrine of God*, pp. 767–72.

able to settle Trinitarian debates to a certain degree through their contribution to the standardization of the language of God as three *hypostases* and one *ousia*—Greek terminology that can be understood as functioning similarly to Tertullian's earlier Latin phrasing of one *substantia* and three *personas*.[37] As Gregory of Nazianzus remarked, "And when I speak of God you must be illumined at once by one flash of light and by three. Three in Individualities or Hypostases, if any prefer so to call them, or persons, for we will not quarrel about names so long as the syllables amount to the same meaning."[38] This contribution, then, was immensely important for the resolution of past Trinitarian difficulties and the achievement of a working settlement that continues to bear fruit today.

In terms of their individual contributions, Basil is often credited with writing one of the first great works on the Holy Spirit. The arguments he employs in this treatise have the distinction of stemming from the context of liturgical space since "it is impossible to worship the Son except in the Holy Spirit" and "it is impossible to call upon the Father except in the Spirit of adoption."[39] As tedious as certain sections of the work are, the result of arguing for varying triadic coordinated doxologies ("glory *to* the Father *with* the Son and *together with* Holy Spirit" in addition to the pattern of rendering "glory *to* the Father *through* the Son *in* the Holy Spirit") is the demonstration that the context of worship already shows that the Spirit is divine alongside the Father and the Son since worship is directed to the Spirit. This feature of Christian worship is possible because of what Christians take to be essential to the Spirit's nature and so work.[40] These are available via some

---

[37]Joseph Lienhard makes the counterintuitive point that the "Cappadocian settlement" of "one ousia, three hypostases" cannot be found in such a form in the Cappadocians but that it is found, ironically, in Augustine, leading him to conclude, "The Cappadocian settlement was in fact formulated by Augustine" (see "Augustine of Hippo, Basil of Caesaria, and Gregory Nazianzen," in Aristotle Papanikolaou and George E. Demacopoulos [eds], *Orthodox Readings of Augustine* [Crestwood, NY: St. Vladimir's Seminary Press, 2008], p. 83).

[38]Oration 39 *(On the Holy Lights)*, 11 *(NPNF2, 7:355)*.

[39]*On the Holy Spirit*, 27 as found in St. Basil the Great, *On the Holy Spirit* (Crestwood, NY: St. Vladimir's Seminary Press, 2001), p. 48.

[40]This order—emphasizing the Spirit's nature and work so as to move to glorification—is registered in Andrew Radde-Gallwitz, *Basil of Caesaria: A Guide to His Life and Doctrine* (Eugene, OR: Cascade, 2012), p. 110.

of Basil's pneumatological emphases, including the tripartite
baptismal formula of Matthew 28[41]—which implies that salvation
comes from the Father, Son, and Holy Spirit[42]—as well as the claim
that the Spirit is the source of sanctification.[43] These features of the
economy of salvation point back to God *in se*, who is constituted
by the eternal mutual indwelling of the three divine hypostases, one
of whom is the Holy Spirit.[44]

Gregory of Nyssa, Basil's brother, is often revered and appreciated
on account of his work in Christian mysticism. Gregory was
unabashedly a clarion for claiming the divinity of the Holy Spirit:
the Father, Son, and Spirit are inseparably God from before the
creation. Within the creation this inseparability is further affirmed
since Gregory believed, "Whatever is morally beautiful, whatever
is good, coming from God as it does through the Son, is completed
by the instrumentality of the Spirit that 'worketh all in all.'"[45]
Because no difference in nature or operation exists in this eternal
fellowship, Father, Son, and Spirit can be called "one God" and
not "three gods." By implication, then, whereas the Spirit is often
associated exclusively with the work of sanctification, one cannot
say that only the Spirit sanctifies if this means that such work is
undertaken separate from the Father and the Son.

The last of the Cappadocians, Gregory of Nazianzus, proclaimed
a number of similar points to his compatriots.[46] For instance, the
indivisibility of the Godhead is elaborated in his oration *On Holy
Baptism* in quite a memorable way: "No sooner do I distinguish
Them than I am carried back to the One. When I think of any One
of the Three I think of Him as the Whole, and my eyes are filled,

---

[41]*On the Holy Spirit*, 24 (p. 45).

[42]*On the Holy Spirit*, 26 (p. 46).

[43]*On the Holy Spirit*, 22 (p. 43).

[44]See Letter 236.6 (NPNF2, 8:278). Basil is reticent in speaking directly of the Spirit's
divinity in *On the Holy Spirit*, but in his letters he is detectably forthright, leading
to the possibility—as Gregory of Nazianzus explicitly believed to be the case—that
Basil was tactfully and rhetorically mindful in his treatise on pneumatology.

[45]*On the Holy Spirit: Against the Macedonians* (NPNF2, 5:324). Also note the similar claim in *On "Not Three Gods"*: "Every operation which extends from God to
the Creation . . . has its origin from the Father, and proceeds through the Son, and is
perfected in the Holy Spirit" (NPNF2, 5:334).

[46]See his oration *On Pentecost*, particularly the eloquent litany of expressions in 9
(NPNF2, 7:382).

and the greater part of what I am thinking of escapes me. I cannot grasp the greatness of that One so as to attribute a greater greatness to the Rest. When I contemplate the Three together, I see but one torch, and cannot divide or measure out the Undivided Light."[47] Of particular importance here is the fifth of his *Theological Orations*, which is devoted principally to the Holy Spirit. Gregory continues with the theme of the inseparability of the Three, claiming this to be from the beginning.[48] In terms of the inner-Trinitarian life, Gregory advances that the procession of the Spirit is distinct from the generation of the Son in the sense that these have presented themselves differently. The meaning of these relations, however, is not altogether clear because they have to do with the mystery of God, but they certainly do not mean differences in essences or actions.[49] Relationality marks God's inner life, and the hypostatic distinctions are to be held in accordance with their manifestation.[50] On this logic, Gregory establishes the distinction to be made of the Spirit: "The Holy Ghost is truly Spirit, coming forth from the Father indeed, but not after the manner of the Son, for it is not by Generation but by Procession (since I must coin a word for the sake of clearness)."[51] Finally, for those who charge that the Spirit is not worshiped outright in Scripture and tradition, Gregory remarks that "it is in the Spirit in whom we worship, and in whom we pray."[52] Gregory continues, "Therefore to adore or to pray to the Spirit seems to me to be simply Himself offering prayer or adoration to Himself."[53]

Augustine and the *filioque* controversy

Many more thinkers could be cited in this survey of the early church's pneumatological reflections, but when one thinks of the

[47]*On Holy Baptism*, 41 (NPNF2, 7:375).
[48]*Theological Orations*, 5.4 (NPNF2, 7:318).
[49]See *Theological Orations*, 3.16 (NPNF2, 7:306–307).
[50]*Theological Orations*, 5.8–9 (NPNF2, 7:320).
[51]Oration 39 *(On the Holy Lights)*, 12 (NPNF2, 7:356).
[52]*Theological Orations*, V.12 (NPNF2, 7:321).
[53]*Theological Orations*, V.12 (NPNF2, 7:321).

immediate aftermath of the Nicene era, one figure towers above
the rest: Augustine of Hippo (354–430). The African father has
repeatedly wielded astonishing influence on the shape of Christianity
since his lifetime for a number of reasons and through a variety of
works, one of those being *On the Trinity*. In this treatise, Augustine
assumes and relies on many claims registered already within fourth-
century developments, particularly those of the Cappadocians.[54] As
noted above, he solidified what has been deemed the Cappadocian
settlement, and interestingly he, like the Nazianzen, was in a certain
way at a loss to substantiate significantly the procession of the
Spirit.[55] Augustine's Trinitarianism is also marked in part by an
emphasis on the inseparable operations of the triune persons as well
as an underlying and constant appreciation for the divine simplicity.
On both of these scores, Augustine is simply embodying features of
what was becoming the "catholic tradition" on such matters.[56]

Augustine is often remembered for the imagery that he
employed to speak of the Trinity and so by implication the Spirit
as well. Augustine's form of elaborating and substantiating the
Trinitarian life was precisely through the use of certain images
and visuals that have generally been received in many different
ways. For instance, he speaks repeatedly of the Spirit as both "gift"
and "love," taking as his cue, among other passages, Romans 5:5
and First John 4:7–16.[57] These ways of speaking of the Spirit's

---

[54]Augustine's reception of the Cappadocians was mediated, but interestingly
(and notoriously) he remarked that he did not understand or found obscure the
Cappadocian distinction between *ousia* and *hypostasis* (*De Trinitate*, 5.2.10 as found
in *The Trinity*, trans. Edmund Hill, O. P. [Brooklyn: New City Press, 1991], p. 196).
I believe people have made too much of what can be taken to be a simple, technical
matter. Clearly, Augustine understood and showed a number of Cappadocian claims
and sensibilities throughout his work.

[55]See Lienhard, "Augustine of Hippo, Basil of Caesaria, and Gregory Nazianzen,"
pp. 84–5.

[56]See the broad treatment in John Behr, "Calling upon God as Father: Augustine
and the Legacy of Nicaea," in Papanikolaou and Demacopoulos (eds), *Orthodox
Readings of Augustine* (Crestwood, NY: St. Vladimir's Seminary Press, 2008),
pp. 153–65.

[57]See *De Trinitate*, 15.5 (pp. 418–26). For an elaboration of this imagery and its
scriptural warrants, see Matthew Levering, "The Holy Spirit in the Trinitarian
Communion: 'Love' and 'Gift?'" *International Journal of Systematic Theology* 16
(2014): 126–42.

identity are important on a number of scores, including that they are "relational terms and have built into them reciprocity and mutuality."[58] At the same time, it should be noted that some believe this interpersonal quality of Augustine's imagery to be compromised because while the personhood of the Father and Son is registered through these analogies, the Spirit's individuation may appear less so. For instance, to take love imagery, the Father is cast as the Lover, the Son as the Beloved, and the Spirit as the Bond of Love (*nexus amoris*) they share. As one can readily sense, a "bond" or "nexus" sounds inherently impersonal. Some believe a kind of depersonalization is also at play in a broader sense via another of Augustine's analogies—the psychological, "single-subject" triad of memory, understanding, and will.

Given Augustine's prominence within Western theology, some have alleged that his influence was formidable in the development of the split between the Western and Eastern churches that culminated in the Great Schism of 1054.[59] Particularly, Augustine has been read as part of a paradigm made famous by Théodore de Régnon in the latter part of the nineteenth century in which the West is depicted as approaching Trinitarianism through an emphasis upon the essence of divinity and moving on to accommodate the diversity of the divine persons whereas the East is cast as predisposed to pursue the opposite.[60] Within this narrative, Augustine is portrayed as the towering figure behind the solidification of the Western alternative. De Régnon's paradigm has especially been prominent functionally in polemic leveled by certain Eastern thinkers over and against the West.[61] As prevalent as this reading of Augustine has been, however, it should be noted that Augustine has not always been received

---

[58]Robert Louis Wilken, *The Spirit of Early Christian Thought: Seeking the Face of God* (New Haven, CT: Yale University Press, 2003), p. 104.

[59]This view needs to be qualified. For instance, Photius of Constantinople—a figure directly related to the exacerbation of the conflict—defended Augustine and believed that Eastern difficulties with Augustine were significantly due to corruptions of his work; see George E. Demacopoulos and Aristotle Papanikolaou, "Augustine and the Orthodox: 'The West' in the East," in Demacopoulos and Papanikolaou (eds), *Orthodox Readings of Augustine*, p. 15.

[60]For a critique of this view, see Michel René Barnes, "Augustine in Contemporary Trinitarian Theology," *Theological Studies* 56 (1995): 237–50.

[61]These would include John Romanides, Christos Yannaras, and John Zizioulas.

this way by the East. Certainly, the East has typically worried
about Augustine's views on sin and grace, especially as they were
formulated by the Bishop of Hippo in the Pelagian controversy; on
this front, the differences between Augustine and the East are fairly
clear and pronounced. But in terms of Trinitarianism, Augustine—as
noted above—falls in line with many Cappadocian and pro-
Nicene sensibilities. Less agonistic climates than those sometimes
characteristic of Western-Eastern exchanges have and could yield
more sensible and careful receptions of Augustine by the East.

One suspects that part of the difficulty with the East's
appropriation of Augustine's Trinitarianism is his support
for what is referred to (perhaps misleadingly) as the "double
procession" of the Spirit,[62] which was subsequently associated
with the term *filioque* ("and the Son") that was added to the
Nicene-Constantinopolitan Creed by the West (so that in the third
article one reads that the Spirit "proceeds from the Father *and
the Son*") and that significantly contributed to the Great Schism.
The addition of the *filioque* seems to have occurred simply by
practice in the West, with a public clarification taking place in the
Council of Toledo in 589. Further solidification of the practice
was reached at the Fourth Synod of Braga in 675. Easterners
took exception to this move through the advocacy of Photius of
Constantinople, whose life spanned most of the ninth century.
In 867 Photius condemned the *filioque* and its predominance
in the West; he believed that proper Spirit-speech should entail
the affirmation that the Spirit proceeds from the Father "alone."
Nevertheless, by papal action, the *filioque* was included in the
Latin form of the Nicene Creed after 1014.

For those not involved directly in these traditions or mindful
of their history, it may be difficult to appreciate all that is at stake
with the addition of the *filioque* to the Nicene Creed. Also, in the
polemic between the East and West, the East oftentimes has focused
on the *filioque* as representative and maybe even at the source of
many of the contested matters and developments between these two

---

[62]Augustine registers the point at many places in *De Trinitate*. One example is found
in 5.3.15: "We must confess that the Father and the Son are the origin of the Holy
Spirit; not two origins, but just as Father and Son are one God, and with reference
to creation one creator and one lord, so with reference to the Holy Spirit they are
one origin" (p. 199).

long-standing traditions.[63] There are plenty of factors to consider
with all that *filioque* has come to represent. We will only consider
a sampling in what follows. On the one hand, the difficulty could
be attributed to the offense of negligence and due process with its
inclusion. In other words, the decision to modify the Creed was
not historically undertaken in a way that all stakeholders had a
say. But theological concerns were also important, and these have
become quite pronounced in the ensuing debates. Put pointedly,
the conceptualization of the inner-Trinitarian life was called into
question with the addition of the *filioque*. The formulation raised
the stakes regarding how the Trinity is most properly and faithfully
related within Christian speech. Theological sensibilities, a guiding
sense of propriety, and nonnegotiable logics have all been involved
in the ongoing controversy.

To briefly summarize the theological stakes, the East believes
Trinitarianism is uniquely secured conceptually by the affirmation of
the hypostatic distinctiveness of each of the triune persons. Therefore,
the Father is distinctly the "fount" or "source" of divinity; the Son is
distinctly generated by the Father; and the Spirit distinctly proceeds
from the Father.[64] This logic both preserves the "monarchy" of
the Father (which was a prominent and long-standing Trinitarian
concern) and maintains an articulation that "personalizes" or
hypostatizes the identity of each of the triune persons along the
lines of relations of origin. The East believes the *filioque* threatens
the uniqueness of the persons by blurring the distinction between
the Father and the Son (since the *filioque* can be taken to mean
that both are a "source" of the Spirit) and by subordinating the
Spirit below the Father and the Son. When framed this way, the
issues appear more serious than simply a wordplay. For the East,
the integrity of Trinitarianism rests on premises that are questioned
or problematized by the inclusion of the *filioque* into the Creed.

---

[63]Vladimir Lossky (rather reductively) opined that the *filioque* was the sole dogmatic
grounds for the separation between the East and the West; see *In the Image and
Likeness of God* (Crestwood, NY: St. Vladimir's Seminary Press, 1974), p. 71.
[64]The language of "procession" really "does not say anything specific about the
Spirit's mode of being" (Bernd Oberdorfer, "The Holy Spirit—A Person?," in Michael
Welker (ed.), *The Work of the Spirit* [Grand Rapids, MI: Eerdmans, 2006], p. 30);
nevertheless, the claim was made so as to at least frame the relationship as distinct
from the Son's eternal generation.

For the West's part, the Son and the Spirit have to be tied in some way within God's inner life. The consubstantiality of the triune persons demands it. Otherwise, two binary relationships would be operative that apparently seem to be on two different tracks, and such a formulation appears to be anything but triune on first blush. To be fair to both sides, a tradition does exist within Christian reflection to say that the Spirit comes from the Father and through the Son, and a number of passages within the NT (e.g. John 14:26, 15:26 and others) suggest that the Son has some role in the missional sending of the Spirit (which for Augustine particularly[65] and the West generally is a valuable point: for these, at least an analogy from the "economic" accounts of God's self-presentation can extend into God's "immanent" life). The question becomes whether *filioque* is capable of expressing such nuancing or if its unqualified form in the Western version of the Creed confuses more than it illuminates.

Obviously, a controversy spanning hundreds of years will continue to persist, particularly one in which sensibilities and propriety sets are both so intricately resisted and sustained.[66] Caricatures at this stage of the conversation are unhelpful, and totalizing narratives such as the de Régnon paradigm should be actively resisted. After all, a figure such as Augustine (who has been brought into this particular conversation repeatedly) is difficult to pin down on matters such as these. The complexity of his thought merits an attentive and careful reception. Take the words of a recent commentator on the Bishop from Hippo: For Augustine, "The Father generates the Son in the act to which he gives rise to the trinitarian communion in the Spirit, the Spirit is given to the

---

[65]Notice what Augustine says in relation to John 20:22, "Not that the physical breath that came from [Jesus'] body and was physically felt was the substance of the Holy Spirit; but it was a convenient symbolic demonstration that the Holy Spirit proceeds from the Son as well as from the Father" (4.5.29) (p. 174). Augustine can say this here while subsequently alluding to what can be termed the *monarchia* of the Father at the end of Book 4.

[66]The topic has been a source of relatively recent ecumenical work; see Lukas Vischer (ed.), *Spirit of God, Spirit of Christ*, Faith and Order Paper No. 103 (London: SPCK, 1981). See also the helpful proposal on offer by Thomas Weinandy in *The Father's Spirit of Sonship: Reconceiving the Trinity* (Eugene, OR: Wipf and Stock, 2010).

Son in order that the Spirit will come forth from the Son."[67] But
notice the ensuing complexity, which Ayres duly notes: "This both
gives and does not give the Son a role in the constitution of the
Spirit. It does give because the Father does not give to the Son a
Spirit as it were 'fully formed' who then comes in some subsequent
act from the Son . . . And yet, the Spirit comes from the Father as
personal and active giving love who gives himself in the Son to the
Father and does so at the Father's breathing."[68] In other words,
Augustine's Trinitarianism is much more complex than those
readings that would locate it in simplistic categories in which it
privileges the "one" over the "three" would have it. By implication,
his views on the double procession of the Holy Spirit are more in
keeping with certain patterns of the "catholic tradition" in which
both the Father and Son have distinct roles to play in the divine
life than a view that would simply diminish the particularity and
so individuation of the three triune persons.

Conclusion

The terrain covered in this chapter is vast. Many scholars have
devoted their academic careers to one figure, movement, or
controversy that was simply noted in passing in this survey. But
if one were to take a "bird's-eye view" of this time period, one
could say that pneumatological developments in the early church
set the stage for a more determinative approach to the Spirit's
identity and work within Christian dogmatics. Patterns, concerns,
and approaches began to be stabilized to some degree after this
time period. To take but one example: Much of what Bernard of
Clairvaux (1090–1153) says regarding the Spirit assumes or extends
the gestures made by Augustine centuries before. Alterations,
innovations, and imaginative reconsiderations have occurred in

---

[67]Lewis Ayres, "*Sempiterne Spiritus Donum*: Augustine's Pneumatology and the
Metaphysics of Spirit," in Papanikolaou and Demacopoulos (eds), *Orthodox
Readings of Augustine*, p. 148.
[68]Ayres, "*Sempiterne Spiritus Donum*," pp. 148–9. One should note also that for all
Augustine says that could be taken as the double procession of the Spirit, he also
make a point to stress that the Spirit proceeds from the Father *principaliter* (or "as
a first principle").

the field of pneumatology after this period, but some stabilizing groundwork—a baseline so to speak—was achieved at this time.

After these two major survey chapters, we move now to consider some critical areas within pneumatological discussions, ones that are oftentimes significantly disputed among academics, ecclesial traditions, and laypeople. Obviously, easy answers are not available in such conversations. What is possible is exposure to the reasons for why such matters are so difficult in the current climate. Therefore, one of the strategies in the following chapters is to prompt some working sense of why these matters are disputed and what is at stake with such conversations. Additionally, however, a path will be anticipated and developed to some degree in each of the chapters, not so as to pretend to "solve" these contested matters but by way of extending the consideration of these issues further within the particularities of specific proposals. The next chapter proceeds as such and is of vital importance for all that follows in the rest of the book in that it considers the deep (and oftentimes implicit) relationship between pneumatological framings and worldview thinking.

4

Spirit and life

Creation and cosmology

"It is the Spirit that gives life"

JOHN 6:63

In the opening words of the Genesis creation accounts, one finds prior to God speaking and creation coming forth that God's spirit/ wind/breath "swept over the face of the waters" (Gen 1:2). Despite this reference, as early and as distinct as it is in this account, Christians have typically looked to God's Word as a more pertinent matter for cosmological concern. Of course, the Johannine witness (John 1 in particular) makes much of a *logos* or "Word" thematic, and Stoic philosophy, one of the dominant philosophical schools of the first-century Mediterranean world, also made use of such language in its own ways. As Christians went on to develop their theological acumen, one of their influences was Philo of Alexandria, who himself employed features of a *logos* framework. Justin Martyr and others of the Apologetic Era went on to formulate what has been deemed a "*logos* christology," which was cast to have cosmological ramifications, as later seen in the work of Maximus the Confessor. This historical emphasis on Christology for cosmological matters raises the question if pneumatology has been neglected as a result: Have any connections been made between pneumatology and cosmology? Is there something to be said about the interrelationship between God's Spirit and the creation at its core?

As noted throughout this book, pneumatological reflection
has consistently lagged behind outright Christological claims
and development, and the same holds true on these matters:
Pneumatology has not enjoyed the same kind of extensive application
to cosmology as Christology has. Nevertheless, some important
points are worth sustaining, especially as related to the long-term
viability and shape of pneumatology. First of all, from the biblical
witness we have already noted the ambiguity potentially at play in
the Bible's usage of *ruach* and *pneuma*. These terms are often used in
relation to both God and the creaturely realm. Such indeterminacy
creates room for constructive possibilities. Furthermore, the creation
account of Genesis 2 makes the explicit point that breath and life
are interrelated: "then the LORD God formed man from the dust of
the ground, and breathed into his nostrils the breath of life; and the
man became a living being" (Gen 2:7). On account of this passage,
the dogmatic pattern is set for the consideration of the link between
God and humanity in terms of breath and the giving of life, both
of which are often tied to the Spirit. From early church traditions,
one of the standout examples of this link is the hymn "Veni Creator
Spiritus," which is often attributed to different figures and which
has a variety of forms. Given its beauty and relevance for this
discussion, the hymn is worth considering extensively. One of its
versions takes the following shape:

Creator-Spirit, all-Divine
Come, visit every soul of Thine,
And fill with Thy celestial flame
The hearts which Thou Thyself didst frame.
O gift of God, Thine is the sweet
Consoling name of Paraclete—
And spring of life and fire and love
And unction flowing from above
The mystic sevenfold gifts are Thine,
Finger of God's right hand divine;
The Father's promise sent to teach
The tongue a rich and heavenly speech.
Kindle with fire brought above
Each sense, and fill our hearts with love;
And grant our flesh, so weak and frail,
The strength of Thine which cannot fail.

Drive far away our deadly foe.
And grant us Thy true peace to know;
So we, led by Thy guidance still,
May safely pass through every ill.
To us, through Thee, the grace be shown
To know the Father and the Son;
And Spirit of Them both, may we
Forever rest our faith in Thee.
To Sire and Son be praises meet,
And to the Holy Paraclete;
And may Christ send us from above
That Holy Spirit's gift of love.[1]

Several key themes from this ancient hymn stand out for the present discussion. Straightaway in the first stanza one sees the affirmation that this Spirit is both God and Creator, thereby establishing this One's right or purchase upon every creature. At the same time, given that the Spirit created all, the Spirit can also "inflame" or "impassion" all. In other words, a dynamism is at play through the use of a Spirit-lens for the Creator-creation interface, one that in this case has resonances with affectivity and desire. This dynamism could also include a number of other possibilities, including the comforting role of the Paraclete, the impartation of the gifts, the enriching of the tongue, and the granting of peace, guidance, and rest. A final quality of this hymn worth mentioning is the way it preserves a working sense of what we have been calling a "pneumatology from below" (given the utilization of creation themes) as well as a "pneumatology from above" (particularly through both the mentioning of "the promise of the Father" and the allusion to Christ sending the Spirit to the disciples). That this hymn keeps both of these perspectives at play is noteworthy.

The time has come, however, for us to pause and nuance these categories we have been using a bit further. The "from below" and "from above" pneumatological designations used throughout this book have been employed as heuristic devices to sustain a perspectival and conceptual differentiation that can be seen in a number of sources, including the biblical materials. They both represent

[1]The version of the "Hymn" cited here is from Robert C. Broderick (ed.), *The Catholic Encyclopedia* (Nashville, TN: Thomas Nelson, 1976), pp. 598–9.

categories worth appropriating so as to elaborate and celebrate features of the Spirit's work. Nevertheless, their rigid maintenance does not permit of some kind of working reconciliation, something which is much needed in discussions interrelating pneumatology and cosmology. Paradigmatically, they stress two different approaches to the Spirit's work, and their persistent bifurcation may lead to the belief that one has to be chosen over and against another. This is always the challenge when binary forms are used in theology: A configuration of two options usually yields formulations and so subsequent appropriations in which one aspect or feature of a pair is privileged over the other. On account of these categorizations, people may be inclined "to pick sides" in what can be framed as a debate for primacy or privilege. Again, conceptually such a move is understandable. On long-term pneumatological grounds, however, the strategy can significantly complicate the search and formulation of an expansive pneumatological portrayal.

As a way of making headway on these matters, I hope to radicalize the possible implications stemming from Paul's claim before the Athenians that "in [God] we live and move and have our being" (Acts 17:28).[2] Whatever the claim's possible extra-Pauline source, its thematic thrust reckons with a cosmological outlook. And given Christian Trinitarian claims—which temporarily allow for a hypostatic focus alongside the claim that the Trinity is one even in God's works in the economy—one could go on to say that it is "in the Spirit" that we live, move, and have our being. The thrust of such reasoning points to a categorical sensibility: The Spirit's activity in the world cannot be communicated by the simple

---

[2] I realize that with the citation of this verse particularly and the language associated with it broadly, the category of "panentheism" is often raised. I have opted to avoid this term because it is exceedingly difficult to circumscribe. For a work that charts various possibilities in its chapters, see Philip Clayton and Arthur Peacocke (eds), *In Whom We Live and Move and Have Our Being: Panentheistic Reflections on God's Presence in a Scientific World* (Grand Rapids, MI: Eerdmans, 2004). I tend to approach this term similarly to a number of Orthodox proposals, particularly Kallistos Ware's. In the collection cited, Ware remarks that panentheism can mean "the belief that God, while *above* the world, is at the same time *within* the world, everywhere present as the heart of its heart, the core of its core" (p. 159, emphasis original); such a broad definition is amenable to the arguments developed in this chapter particularly and this book on a whole.

categories of "below" and "above," for even on this score, the Spirit transcends and goes beyond this particular dyad.

In what follows, we will consider a topic that has increasingly been at the forefront of such cosmological discussions, namely the interrelationship between pneumatology and science. After this line of exploration, we will move to evaluate the theme of creation dogmatically from a pneumatological perspective so as to propose features tied to the theme's dogmatic purchase.

The Spirit and science

By way of setting up the next chapter, let us say that the Spirit's primary form of activity is to work through the world as we know it: On countless occasions, the Spirit is talked about in the Bible and among the faithful as working through persons, events, and things. If that affirmation is compelling, then it requires some working sense of what the world is and how it is ordered. These operable assumptions press upon ontological/metaphysical claims, ones that are indelibly shaped by the predominant scientific paradigm at play in a given context. Ever since Thomas Kuhn's *The Structure of Scientific Revolutions*, contemporary science has been portrayed for what it is: one paradigm or framework of many possibilities by which to interpret data.[3] As history has shown, when enough pressure or a sufficient number of outliers push against a regnant scientific framework, the scientific model has to change so as to account for the mounting counterevidence. The history of science has shown us repeatedly that cosmological outlooks are provisional and transitory. Science is largely paradigmatic, and paradigm shifts necessarily take place over time.

In terms of today, science, as we typically understand it, is shaped by a variety of naturalistic assumptions. As difficult as it may be to establish in the minds of many, naturalism is but one scientific paradigm in the global history of ideas, and given its particularities and scope as well as the overall complexity of reality, it cannot account for all things observed. As Cornelius Hunter has argued

---

[3]See Thomas S. Kuhn, *The Structure of Scientific Revolutions*, 3rd edition (Chicago: University of Chicago Press, 1996).

in terms of naturalism's locality: "There is no experiment or proof that demonstrates that naturalism is the source of everything we observe. It is possible that nonnaturalistic phenomena exist, and it is not a good sign that this needs explaining."[4] Hunter argues for describing science as it is typically pursued as subscribing to what he calls "theological naturalism." This particular account of naturalism relies not on empirical findings for its legitimacy and extensiveness of reach but rather on metaphysical reasoning in that it assumes for itself the power to describe and explain not only how things are and work but also how they came to be. Therefore, when science is confronted with its inadequacy or inability to explain something, the assumption at work in this particular version is that "the correct naturalistic solution has not yet been found."[5] By setting itself up with this kind of limitation, science today—to the degree that it subscribes to "theological naturalism" as Hunter defines it—operates with a self-imposed "blind spot." As Hunter proceeds to say, "science has no mechanism to detect the possibility of nonnatural phenomena. It does not consider the likelihood that a phenomenon might not be purely naturalistic."[6] Given its comprehensive scope, this alternative sounds fideistic with its speculative and yet dogged perpetuation. This quality is why Hunter goes on to use the qualifier "theological" to describe this particular form.

One linguistic way to account for outlying data would be the use of the term "supernaturalism," but notice how such wording already sets up an unhelpful dyad or binary, one between "naturalism" and "supernaturalism." This construal can also fall into the privileging associated with dyadic depictions (and in this case, "naturalism" is the preferred baseline or foundation and "supernaturalism" as a result is marginalized to the periphery). Further, as Hunter notes in his proposals, the baseline itself is not entirely clear or self-aware of both its limits as well as its substance or guiding orientation.

James K. A. Smith has tried to delineate naturalism and does so differently yet complementarily to Hunter. Smith has proposed two forms that are particularly predominant today: reductionistic and

---

[4]Cornelius G. Hunter, *Science's Blind Spot: The Unseen Religion of Scientific Naturalism* (Grand Rapids, MI: Brazos, 2007), p. 43.
[5]Hunter, *Science's Blind Spot*, p. 44.
[6]Hunter, *Science's Blind Spot*, p. 45.

nonreductionistic naturalism.[7] As to the first, reductionistic naturalism advocates a kind of physicalism in that all entities in the universe are understood as material and physical. Quite simply, within this view, nothing other than those sorts of things exists; supernatural phenomena, therefore, are out of the question as possibilities. The second kind—nonreductionistic naturalism—is not as trenchant or expansive as the reductionist sort; it will allow for a divinity that is a vitalizing, immanent principle in the world's outworking in some panentheistic construal—as long as this outworking subscribes to the "laws of nature." However, nonreductionistic naturalism is also weary of accounts of supernaturalism. In fact, after his brief survey, Smith concludes that what often binds these two naturalisms in particular and others generally is a common rejection of a certain form of supernaturalism, that is, the "interventionist" variety in which supernatural phenomena temporarily interrupt, alter, or suspend the baseline of naturalism that allegedly provides the conditions necessary for scientific inquiry.[8] Dominant features of naturalism in this presentation would be the predictive, cause-and-effect regularities that are empirically observable and verifiable.[9] The shared assumption would be that interventionism involves an exception to how the world typically and reliably works. Therefore, defining supernaturalism in an interventionist way functionally marginalizes its relevance and applicability. In this sense, naturalisms are usually very clear in what they are not: Naturalisms cannot accommodate an interventionist supernaturalism since this would be a threat to the way they are usually formulated. Outside of these broad strokes, however, naturalisms are less inclined to demonstrate what they

---

[7] See his survey in James K. A. Smith, *Thinking in Tongues: Pentecostal Contributions to Christian Philosophy* (Grand Rapids, MI: Eerdmans, 2010), beginning on p. 90.

[8] Elsewhere, Smith wishes to draw a distinction between science and naturalism. For him, "science" is "a set of practices for empirically investigating and explaining natural phenomena" whereas "naturalism" is usually a viewpoint or orientation that is assumed so as to make data intelligible. As it will be noted below, given its penchant for delving into the metaphysical, "naturalism" is best understood as a worldview. See his "Is There Room for Surprise in the Natural World? Naturalism, the Supernatural, and Pentecostal Spirituality," in James K. A. Smith and Amos Yong (eds), *Science and the Spirit* (Bloomington: Indiana University Press, 2010), p. 37. As this delineation makes clear, one can do science without subscribing to naturalism per se.

[9] Smith, *Thinking in Tongues*, pp. 91, 94. This "regulatory principle" is often taken to suggest that its law-like patterns mean there are no exceptions to its forms (Smith, "Is There Room for Surprise," p. 39).

claim positively.[10] From the form of this presentation, it would seem that the reductive and nonreductive kinds are metaphysical in nature, and in being so, they represent not simply scientific assumptions but very much premises of an operative worldview. Smith denotes with "metaphysical" what Hunter largely does with "theological."[11]

With this dyadic presentation of the natural-supernatural divide and its implicit privileging of the natural as the orientation for understanding "how the world is," the framework is set for a dyadic presentation of not only the faith-science dialogue but potentially also the theological task itself, including—and most pressingly for our case—the role of the Spirit within the processes of the cosmos. Smith points out that if what is deemed the "natural" is the baseline, then the theological side of the science-theology exchange will necessarily subscribe to a correlationist paradigm in which theology "fills in gaps" or "finds spaces" to have some relevance in the broader naturalistic scheme.[12] Theologians oftentimes assume these "rules to the game" in faith-science discussions, not so as to give up on their theological orientations per se (at least explicitly) but more likely because in these interactions such is oftentimes deemed "the price of admission for scientific respectability."[13]

One of the significant contributions on this score by Smith is that he is willing to grant that just as there are a number of naturalisms, there may also be other forms of supernaturalism besides the interventionist variety. One way of framing what he is after is to alter the operational assumptions in these discussions: Rather than starting from the baseline of a specific naturalism per se, he calls for a reconfiguration of the categories so that naturalism and supernaturalism—as they typically traffic—are not antithetically

---

[10]Smith, *Thinking in Tongues*, p. 92.

[11]One should also note that there is such a view as "methodological naturalism," which is essentially pragmatic and functional in nature and so agnostic on the metaphysical front (see Smith, "Is There Room for Surprise," pp. 40–2). Hunter traces this tradition to the work of Francis Bacon. As amenable as this approach is to multiple worldviews, it seems that the more prevalent model within scientific communities and popular understandings would be the metaphysical forms; that is why the latter have received the bulk of attention in this chapter.

[12]Smith, *Thinking in Tongues*, p. 94. And of course, when those gaps are themselves explicable on naturalistic grounds, then no God is needed (see Hunter, *Science's Blind Spot*, p. 48).

[13]Smith, *Thinking in Tongues*, p. 95.

depicted. In some sense, what is needed is nothing short of a new language to account for a different kind of ontology, one that does not subscribe to nature's emancipation through demythologization so as to yield a kind of reductive disenchantment with the way things are. Smith's linguistic preferences would be possibilities along the lines of an "enchanted naturalism" or an "en-Spirited naturalism."[14] Obviously, for purposes of this study, the latter phrasing would be ideal as a gesture hinting at a way out of this conceptual entrenchment.

Inherent to Smith's proposals is a pneumatological worldview, one which he simply labels "pentecostal," but he is clear to note that the term is more expansive for him than simply the revivalist forms of Christianity emerging in the twentieth century; he explains, "By 'pentecostal' I mean to refer not to a classical or denominational definition, but rather to an understanding of Christian faith that is radically open to the continued operations of the Spirit."[15] Smith elaborates this pneumatological worldview through five distinct points, the first three of which include a radical openness to God so that God can do something altogether different or new, an "enchanted" theology of creation that understands it as "charged" with the Spirit, and a nondualistic endorsement of both embodiment and materiality (in which these are not considered basically evil but rather—given Smith's other proposals—good on account of the fundamental qualities inherent to the category of creaturehood).[16] As constituents of a worldview, Smith's pentecostal or pneumatological proposals stand in necessary tension with metaphysical naturalisms; they are both vying for the same metaphysical space as they are typically construed. Furthermore, both involve claims that are in some sense religious because each demonstrates "a fundamental commitment to a particular story about reality made on the basis of faith."[17]

---

[14]Smith, *Thinking in Tongues*, p. 97.

[15]Smith, *Thinking in Tongues*, p. xvii.

[16]See Smith's summary in *Thinking in Tongues*, p. 12.

[17]Smith, "Is There Room for Surprise," p. 42. Obviously, some will take strong exception to Smith here, but his point is rather compelling: Metaphysical naturalism is not a claim derived from science; it is a fundamental commitment more akin to faith than science because it cannot be proven on empirical grounds.

It is no wonder, then, that the Holy Spirit is often marginal to Christian thought-forms and speech-practices, for it could very well be the case that different cosmological outlooks are operative in Christian discourse as it is perpetuated by varying constituencies. If Christians assume certain claims at a fundamental level—that is, those that pertain to making sense of how the world is and how it works—the pneumatological possibilities necessarily vary as a result. Just taking inventory of the possibilities across Christianity's many forms, one can see that Christians have demonstrated variety on these scores and in turn different outcomes have come about as a result. On first blush, certain ecclesial and theological traditions simply emphasize and employ Spirit-speech more so than others, and these differences may not simply be due to the ability of some groups to "balance" or "adequately diversify" their theological proposals more so than others. The difference may be attributable to something more basic: rival accounts of "how the world works."

From another angle, one must venture to say something positively about what Smith deems an "en-Spirited naturalism." Here, I join his call by offering very broad orienting proposals to substantiate the claims pertaining to this chapter and the next. Essentially, a reversal of sorts is needed: Rather than making the "supernatural" peripheral, the task requires putting it at the center, thereby problematizing not only the place of privilege that regnant naturalisms enjoy but also calling into question the way the terms have traditionally been defined. A certain kind of imaginative playmaking is necessary here, one that takes on the received patterns and terms so as to reconfigure them for the sake of alternative arrangements and possibilities. In short: I wish to press that *Spirit-matters are the most natural things there are.* Or to put it another way: *Nature is Spirit-graced to its core so that what is fundamentally characteristic of nature is that it is Spirit-related.*[18] If these claims hold, then "interventionism"

---

[18]This claim is made with an openness regarding *how* this state of affairs is the case. One can assume that as scientific paradigms change and shift over time that different models will come to the fore as possible illustrative mechanisms. One such possibility is Wolfhart Pannenberg's pneumatological proposals from field theory. The difficulty, of course, is that as these models change in terms of their own internal viability so may their usefulness or applicability. The "how," then, of this assertion is provisional and open for ongoing possibilities; nevertheless, the claim itself can stand independently of these models as a working dogmatic premise.

is illogical in that *the natural is itself miraculous*. Taken together, these claims require nothing short of a radicalization of the doctrine of creation as it oftentimes is appropriated by both scientists and theologians alike. This move is in keeping with how theology is a faith-conditioned discourse that attempts to narrate the world coherently on its own terms while simultaneously maintaining a dialogical and open disposition to other narrations and disciplinary orientations. But the main point to pursue here is that the Spirit's operations—however these appear in terms of gifts/fruit of the Spirit, providence, inspiration/illumination, miracles, prophecy, and so on—are, on Christian terms, *natural* and so *normal*; they are part of the world as Christians understand it—or at least, I would contend, how they ought to understand it.

Obviously, these claims can be controversial, even on theological grounds. A number of Christian traditions have assumed a "naturalized" quality for empirical reality, whether this be in terms of readings of revelatory history (in which, for example, the "extraordinary" charismata are said to be only properly manifest and available during certain dispensations or epochs because of their exceptional quality), sacraments (in which the elements maintain a naturalized baseline so as to maintain their material integrity), and a host of other topics (not the least of which would be Christology). However, if one were to approach reality in a Scripture-bound and Scripture-inflected kind of way—the kind of approach in which "the text absorbs the world" so to speak—then one is left with the prospect that the happenings of revelatory history and the confessions and experiences of the church (especially in the West's premodern period and in varying contexts throughout the Global South today) point in the direction of a God-tinged, Spirit-infused reality.[19] What is being envisioned here is nothing short of a distinct worldview or imaginary, one that has at its core what can be deemed a "sacramental ontology."[20]

There are different ways to breathe life into these basic orienting claims. Smith particularly finds Radical Orthodoxy's participatory

---

[19]Smith occasionally uses the language that creation is primed for the Spirit's action (*Thinking in Tongues*, pp. 101, 103).
[20]For more on this notion from an explicitly evangelical perspective, see Hans Boersma, *Heavenly Participation: The Weaving of a Sacramental Tapestry* (Grand Rapids, MI: Eerdmans, 2011).

ontology as a resource to articulate this understanding.[21] One of the strategies of those associated with this movement is to go back to premodern sources to account for how the Creator and creation can intersect in vitalizing ways, and they are prompted to do so largely through the earlier movement known as *nouvelle théologie*. One of the figureheads of this French movement was Henri de Lubac, and a major feature of his research agenda was to question precisely the super/natural divide, as first registered in his work *Surnaturel*. Although de Lubac had his own context in mind when making his claims (one that had him opposed to a neo-Thomist perspective), his claims were such that they are apropos here: The cosmos, in being creation, is already tinged and constituted by God's self. From the creaturely side, then, to be and to thrive is to participate in God's economy and so in some sense in God's own life. Smith highlights the logic this way: "On the one hand, [this participatory ontology] affirms that matter *as created* exceeds itself and *is* only insofar as it participates in or is suspended from the transcendent Creator; on the other hand, it affirms that there is a significant sense in which the transcendent inheres in immanence."[22]

If creation is understood as pneumatologically shaped and constituted, then a range of descriptive possibilities can follow. The regular and reliable aspects of the empirical realm can be narrated as properly Spirit-shaped and Spirit-charged. Such a possibility has already been registered with metaphors and language associated with the Spirit. For instance, Hildegard von Bingen associated the Spirit's work with the "greening" effect of nature; in her way of thinking, the Spirit is not only *vita* but also *viriditas*.[23] Also, miracles need not be cast in an interventionist fashion but in terms of "intensities of participation" in an already Spirit-drenched world.[24] Fruition, cultivation, maturation—these can all be considered as Spirit-prompted, Spirit-guided, and Spirit-directed. In short, under

[21]Smith explores this movement more in *Introducing Radical Orthodoxy: Mapping a Post-Secular Theology* (Grand Rapids, MI: Baker Academic, 2004).

[22]Smith, *Thinking in Tongues*, p. 100.

[23]See an elaboration of this metaphor of Hildegard in Elizabeth Dreyer, *Holy Power, Holy Presence: Rediscovering Medieval Metaphors for the Holy Spirit* (New York: Paulist Press, 2007), pp. 85–6.

[24]See Smith, *Thinking in Tongues*, p. 102. See also Smith's article, "The Spirit, Religions, and the World as Sacrament," *Journal of Pentecostal Theology* 15.2 (2007): 251–61.

this orientation Christians can both worship and see the Spirit's presence and work not so much as coming from outside of the physical world in some interventionist fashion but in other, more "naturalized" ways within the creation's ongoing constitution.

The need for a pneumatological cosmology

The relationship between pneumatology and cosmology is crucial because so much is allowed or disallowed in pneumatological discussions because of assumptions directly tied to this basic level of consideration. And because these matters are pneumatological, they also have a direct bearing on portrayals of what the Christian life is deemed to look like. Reinhard Hütter has commented in a survey chapter of the Christian life that Christians can largely agree on the "big-ticket" items of Christianity, those that have been established and refined through conciliar consideration, but once the discussion moves to the "Christian life's salient aspects," any working consensus breaks down "rather abruptly."[25] Put another way, most Christians across the globe have some working sense of basic Christian beliefs as represented in creedal materials, but when they move to speak of what constitutes the Christian life—including its call, possibilities, and shape—differences (and mutually exclusive ones at that!) make their way quickly to the forefront.

Why the immediate tensions and disunity on this score? One strong possibility is that a vision of the Christian life relies on an intricate set of plausibility structures that are constituted by some basic, worldview-related convictions. Elsewhere, I have labeled these as "Ur-commitments" alongside the notion of "primordial logics," the latter suggesting the way these fundamental assumptions are put together in a meaning-generating manner.[26] Both these "Ur-commitments" and "primordial logics" usually operate at the

---

[25]Reinhard Hütter, "The Christian Life," in John Webster, Kathryn Tanner, and Iain Torrance (eds), *The Oxford Handbook of Systematic Theology* (Oxford: Oxford University Press, 2007), p. 285.
[26]See Daniel Castelo, "The Spirit, Creaturehood and Sanctification," *International Journal of Systematic Theology* 16.2 (2014): 177–91.

unconscious or even pre-cognitive register since they often are not explicitly brought to the fore but simply picked up from one's wider surroundings through implicit authorities and didactic forces. They are bequeathed to their espousers by wider social formations that narrate overall "how the world works," and in the case of faith, "how Christianity works." Because they are so embedded into one's thought-processes, they are especially difficult to identify, much less question. Commitments regarding the Christian faith generally and the possibilities and shape for the Christian life particularly are often held derivatively from these more basic considerations.

If these are some of the qualities of the current pneumatological state of affairs, then several evaluative remarks are in order. First, if Christians throughout the world operate with some considerable differences at the level of "Ur-commitments" and "primordial logics," then one could plausibly say that these represent fundamentally different ways to pursue the life that is at once commonly labeled "Christian." These differences do not represent varying opinions on this or that matter per se; rather, they constitute alternative ways to imagine and pursue this way of life. Perhaps unsettlingly (although readily notable when specific examples are brought to the fore), these differences could be taken to suggest that "Christianity" can denote distinct—maybe even irreconcilable—visions, strategies, and forms of life. Such observations are important so that the differences spanning Christian embodiment can be reckoned with seriously—hopefully to such a point that their logics might be exposed and their consequences evaluated. If basic commitments regarding "how the world works" are behind a significant portion of Christian differences, then no amount of exegesis or dialogue undertaken at the superficial level will necessarily win the day. The pre-faith-commitments behind the more visible faith-commitments compromise development and progress at the ecumenical and dialogical level, especially if the former are not outright considered in and of themselves.

These many matters have an inestimably significant impact on the state of pneumatology in a given setting. Scholars are prone to say that pneumatology for centuries was neglected or unavailable in the West. I would venture to say that the main culprit here is not necessarily blatant ignorance (as if people forgot or did not know about the Spirit during different time periods). Rather, Westerners in certain places and at certain periods seemingly created a world for themselves in which pneumatology just did not make sense in another way besides an interventionist, "coming-from-the-outside" logic, which in turn marginalized the Spirit and so made pneumatology largely irrelevant for how reality holds together. Put quaintly, many traditions neglect the Spirit because they feel they do not need the Spirit for making sense of their lives. If such is the case, then one cannot help but alarmingly note how this situation is markedly different from the pneumatological cadences surrounding the life of faith as depicted in the testimony of Scripture and various expressions of the Christian church beyond such immediate environs.

A second concern stemming from this contemporary condition is the availability and shape of certain matters directly related to Christian speech and the Christian life. The stakes involved do not simply pertain to whether miracles and prophetic utterances are available today (as important as those concerns are). More fundamentally, basic Christian commitments are implicated in this dynamic as a result. For instance, take the question of transformation. Can people be fundamentally reconstituted and made anew by the presence and work of the Holy Spirit? Certainly, various traditions will have different accounts of what life in Christ might look like, but these differences can be traced back to even more basic commitments related to the Creator-creation interface. The identity and basic constitution of creaturehood, the nature and extent of the fall, the availability and shape of holiness in the believer's life, the role of human agency in the midst of the Trinity's providential work within the economy, the ethos and end of ecclesial life—these and many more are inescapably tinged by "Ur-commitments" and "primordial logics." All the dogmatic loci (including creation, fall, Christology, salvation, sanctification, and eschatology) are influenced in one way or another by what believers ultimately assume is and is not possible in the world as it is understood to be constituted. Without a recognized active role for the Spirit with regard to what reality is, one cannot help but assume that much of what pertains to the Christian "take on things" (as evidenced by a number of resources in the Christian faith) is simply off the table.

Given the shape of this book so far, perhaps the reader can anticipate how this chapter will conclude. In light of the field's indeterminacy, its capacity to deconstruct dyads and binaries, its multiple registers accounting for the totality of human experience, and more, pneumatology can render an alternative account for "how the world works"—and so "how the Christian faith works"—from what might be assumed by prevalent and popular narratives, particularly those in certain parts of the West. To appreciate this point, one may have to be dispositionally amenable to be muted, to be chastened and humbled, to be surprised—in short to have one's "world turned upside down" by the various means the Spirit uses (Acts 17:6) in order to see what it increasingly means to participate more fully in the claim to live, move, and have one's being in the Spirit. Such might be an unsettling, maybe even scary, prospect to some. But then again, how could study and pursuit of the Holy Spirit be otherwise?

5

In the Spirit

Mediation and the economy of sanctification

*"He whom God has sent speaks the words of God,
for he gives the Spirit without measure"*

JOHN 3:34

*"This is the Spirit of truth, whom the world cannot receive,
because it neither sees this One nor knows this One.
You know this One, because this One abides with you,
and this One will be in you"*

JOHN 14:17

The importance of the last chapter for setting up this one cannot be overestimated. However the Spirit is located within the Creator-creation interface will in turn determine the shape of what one goes on to say about the Spirit's presence and work in the world. For many, an interventionist, "from above" approach to Spirit-matters is quite natural, yet one of the specific strategies in this book has been to locate the Holy Spirit in the mundane and the material as well as within ordinary time and quotidian existence. Part of the rationale for this alternative strategy rests on the esotericism that naturally comes with an interventionist logic, which in turn marginalizes and pushes to the periphery all things Spirit-related. This last tendency, as it is readily found, is in tension with varying depictions of the role of the Spirit in the Christian life. Paul hints at the centrality of such a role when he remarks to the Romans, "But you are not in the flesh; you are in the Spirit, since the Spirit of God dwells in you. Anyone who does not have the Spirit of God does not belong to him" (Rom 8:9). For Paul here as well as the thrust of Scripture and church tradition broadly, the Spirit is crucial to the way the Christian life is understood, embodied, and pursued.

Such a claim was registered quite early in formal pneumatological discussions. If we may recall a previous chapter, pivotal to Athanasius's arguments against the *Tropikoi* was to advance the claim that the Spirit's proper work is to make creatures holy so that they could in turn participate in God's life. At this point, Athanasius uses a similar logic to what he advanced in the realm of Christology, namely that the Spirit's work of sanctification (as well as the Son's work of redemption) is the kind of activity that only God could undertake. In other words, the Spirit sanctifies, which is properly and so exclusively the work of a holy God. Within the domain of this claim is the understanding that the goal of the Christian life is to become God-like. For Athanasius and others, the work of sanctification was crucial because this theme involved the healing and shaping of creatures to acquire their true end. At play here is the master-notion of deification or *theosis*.

How does God's Spirit make people holy as God is holy (Lev 19:2; 1 Pet 1:16)? Put another way, how can the economy of sanctification be understood? If the creation is already charged by and primed for the Spirit, then the economy of sanctification should not be considered over and against the created realm but in and through it. One particular movement within the contemporary theological climate has taken this tack, and so it will be mined below. Once this movement has been considered for its pneumatological contribution, the particular topic of Scripture will be broached since Christians attribute special significance to the Bible in the shaping of how the Christian life is expressed and understood.

A pneumatologically constituted canonical heritage

On the contemporary scene, a movement spearheaded by William J. Abraham has come to the fore. Abraham labels this movement "canonical theism" to distinguish it from the more general notion of "philosophical theism." Canonical theism is explicitly historical, ecclesial, and pneumatological in its orientation; its proponents claim a prominent role for the Holy Spirit in time, within people, and through institutions, offices, and materials for bringing to realization God's purposes of salvation and healing. Its broad aims involve the quest "to find an expression of the [Christian] faith that nourishes the soul and that provides shape and motivation for lively involvement in the life and ministry of the church."[1] For this reason, the initiative can help flesh out what mediation might look like in pneumatological focus.

The use of the term "canonical" for Abraham was first registered in his celebrated and oft-discussed *Canon and Criterion in Christian Theology* and developed more fully in the book eponymously titled with the movement itself. According to Abraham, "canons" are means of grace recognized by the church as those "various materials, persons and practices which function to reconnect human agents with their divine source and origin. They are akin to medicine designed to heal and restore human flourishing."[2] Within the heading of "means of grace" could fall a number of spiritual disciplines (prayer, fasting, meditation, and so on) which would require on their own terms a particular synergistic ordering. The term "means of grace" is largely understood in a Wesleyan sense here; they are God-ordained, active forms of waiting for God's presence.[3] They involve human activity no doubt but in such a way that they are best understood as requiring an "active passivity" within a broader "responsive" or "reactive" mode to the prevenient work of the Trinity. The human

---

[1]William J. Abraham, "The Emergence of Canonical Theism," in William J. Abraham, Jason E. Vickers, and Natalie B. Van Kirk (eds), *Canonical Theism: A Proposal for Theology and the Church* (Grand Rapids, MI: Eerdmans, 2008), p. 141.
[2]William J. Abraham, *Canon and Criterion in Christian Theology* (Oxford: Oxford University Press, 1998), p. 1.
[3]For the most sustained treatment of this topic within this particular church tradition, see Henry H. Knight III, *The Presence of God in the Christian Life: John Wesley and the Means of Grace* (Metuchen, NJ: Scarecrow Press, 1992).

side of the dynamic is important when ordered appropriately: God commands and expects something from humans, and their call is to obey and follow. When pursued and lived into positively, this interplay (which is best understood in terms of the logic inherent to covenant arrangements) leads to human flourishing and happiness.

Abraham expands this idea in his second book by speaking of a "canonical heritage" that would include such ecclesial resources as doctrine, saints, church fathers and mothers, liturgies, bishops, councils, icons, and many more.[4] These resources are set apart by God's Spirit so as to help the church grow and mature in its terrestrial sojourning. Rather than a collection of isolated or irrelevant historical artifacts, Abraham and his colleagues see this canonical heritage as one that is rich with possibility in terms of shaping and substantiating Christian witness across time. When taken together, the means of grace and the canonical heritage of the church suggest one basic notion to Abraham: "For canonical theism the core of the faith is not scripture, or creed, or liturgy, or this or that great voice from the past, and the like. The core is the great gift of medicinal salvation mediated through the great canonical heritage of the church, the marvelous, manifold, developmental work of the Holy Spirit before and after Pentecost."[5] The Spirit gifts the church over time with a number of persons, materials, and practices that can be appropriated in an in-Spirited way for the sustenance, formation, and fortification of their lives and witness.

There are many aspects to canonical theism's programmatic proposals, but one detectably strong feature is that it relies heavily on an account of mediation. Since the church's founding, the Spirit has not so much interrupted or intervened artificially in the world's processes as much as worked in time through agents, things, and events to bring about and call forth vestiges of the kingdom. To lead the Christian life involves participating in a way of being that is graced by the Spirit's presence and activity to its very core. In this life, then, gifts stem from the triune God for the people of God with the goal or end that they may heal and flourish before God in one grand, worshipful gesture. Spiritual disciplines, the sacraments, creeds, bishops—these and many other features of the church's "canonical heritage" represent ways in which the Spirit moves in and through the church for the world's

---

[4]See Abraham, "Canonical Theism: Thirty Theses," in *Canonical Theism*, p. 2.
[5]Abraham, "Introduction," in *Canonical Theism*, p. xvi.

redemption and healing. This claim does not mean that the sheer acts of enunciating prayers, partaking of the sacraments, reading sacred texts, or the declarations of bishops will necessarily involve all the many purposes associated with God's ordaining them. After all, the language of mediation is crucial so that there is an abiding, categorical distinction between God and the gifts of God. The arrangement need not be understood in terms of conflation or rivalry. Quite the contrary, the Creator naturally and fittingly works in and through this One's creation in a way that dignifies the creation and discloses the abiding presence and character of the Creator.

Dimensions of holiness

Implicit in these many considerations regarding a "canonical heritage" is also a basic understanding of sanctification, the act by which something is made holy. How is holiness to be understood broadly, and why is it fitting to speak of sanctification as properly a work of God's Spirit? Holiness is a term that is exceedingly cumbersome and difficult to pin down in the contemporary situation, no doubt in part because of a general malaise regarding religious hypocrisy. As soon as "holiness" or "the holy" traffics and is circulated in casual (and even formally theological) conversation, a deep suspicion typically emerges since the language implies a kind of preeminence that works against a number of sensibilities, including political and religious ones.[6] To take the last point, different ecclesial communions consider holiness in sundry ways that in turn exhibit tensions across their many forms.[7] Once again, these differences usually operate out of fundamental commitments related to the Creator-creation interface as these apply to the possibilities and shape for the Christian life. There is simply no way to build a consensus when Ur-commitments

---

[6]For a head-on discussion of these concerns and alternatives to many of the theme's caricatures, see the essays in Daniel Castelo (ed.), *Holiness as a Liberal Art* (Eugene, OR: Pickwick, 2012).

[7]One simple example can prove the point quite expediently: the viability and logic of "sainthood." For some traditions, it is understood that certain notable figures from the past should be remembered and venerated for their contribution to an ongoing, "living" tradition. For others, the category of sainthood falsely privileges some people over others, which in their minds contributes to church division and a false sense of the human condition as it is experienced currently in this "time between the times."

and primordial logics are at odds with one another. One way out of this morass of contention is to survey each of the possible ways holiness can be understood in a variety of theological and church-related belief structures. Some of these possibilities no doubt can be anticipated in light of the pertinent claims made in the previous chapters of this work. But another tack is simply to outline a constructive proposal that inevitably can count on being both resonant and in tension with the options that are available. It is this last approach that will be pursued in the following.

To begin, two general aspects of holiness are worth keeping in tandem. On the one hand, there is the notion of "being set apart" for God's purposes. The implied differentiation with such a move need not (although it subsequently can) carry overtones of qualitative valuation. In other words, something set apart for specific service or roles within the economy of God's purposes need not imply that all else not set apart is somehow less valuable, but it does suggest that with this distinction a break of sorts is involved. Accounting for such a break would necessarily involve mention of the divine prerogative. God chose Jacob rather than Esau, the tribe of Levi as priests instead of any of the other tribes of Israel, and so forth. At the same time, God's purposes may not be carried out by these entities once God sets them apart for special purposes. The process of setting apart may not play out as God intended given the participatory requirements associated with a corresponding covenant partner. The example of Israel's covenant unfaithfulness is one such broad example of this possibility, and the particular cases of Nadab and Abihu, Saul, Jonah, and others fit the bill. In short, holiness involves a kind of differentiation that can include a number of varying, covenant-tinged dynamics from both God's side and the human side of the arrangement.

Whereas the first aspect of holiness (tied to separation and renunciation as it is) may be considered a "negative" connotation overall, a "positive" dimension relates to the way life is pursued and lived out in a determinate way for purposes of healing and flourishing.[8] This second aspect can be extended all the way to the ontological and

---

[8]These two notions can roughly correspond to the dynamics of *mortificatio* and *vivificatio*, ones helpfully elaborated in relation to this theme by John Webster; see *Holiness* (Grand Rapids, MI: Eerdmans, 2003). For an appreciative and yet more expansive take on Webster's proposals, see Daniel Castelo, "Holiness *Simpliciter*," *Wesleyan Theological Journal* 47.2 (2012): 147–64.

creaturely level: Humans were created *as* holy. The divine imprint upon the creaturely realm dignifies creation in that all that a holy God makes is holy on account of its origin and end in a holy God. From another, complementary perspective, humans are called *to be* holy. This perspective is performative in character and does justice to the way humans can lead their lives in one way or another. In this last sense, a holy life can be pursued because a holy God makes such a life possible. Holiness within this framing is intricately tied to the categories of goodness and beauty, both of which are typically "transcendentals" that characterize first and foremost God's own life. On Christian terms, to lead a holy life suggests to lead a good and beautiful life. There are depth dimensions to Christian existence, and when disciples go on to participate in the world with such fullness, they are embracing not only the divine imperative but also the divine provision that makes joyous, happy, and meaningful lives available here and now. Of course, part of this positive dimension to holiness can only be registered eschatologically. For this reason, these holy, good, beautiful lives are complicated by living within an "already-not yet" situation. Nevertheless, the "first-fruits" of the kingdom should be claimed for what they are: Holy signs of a holy God's impending holy reign among God's holy people.

On both counts (i.e. the "negative" and "positive" dimensions), the Spirit plays a crucial role. Because of the Spirit's active work in the economy, people are called, capacitated, and empowered to lead holy lives in the various ways that pertain to such a process. Such work is fittingly and properly the work of God's Spirit. From one side, the Spirit calls people to pursue God's work in the world. The Spirit is a beckoning Spirit, One who calls and sets apart. When this process involves renunciation and pulling away from the lures and temptations of this life, the Spirit can empower through capacitated judgment and fortified resolution.[9] On the other side, the Spirit is the Spirit of truth, goodness, and beauty; therefore, following the prompts

---

[9]It is a fascinating feature of the synoptic gospel tradition that the Spirit is involved in the developments surrounding Jesus' temptation. For instance, Jesus was led by the Spirit (Matt 4:1) and driven out into the wilderness by the Spirit (Mark 1:12). As typically is the case, Luke's explicit Spirit-references shine here as well: Prior to the temptation Jesus was "full of the Holy Spirit" (Luke 4:1), and after the ordeal—to which he had been led by the Spirit to face—he returned to Galilee at once "filled with the power of the Spirit" (Luke 4:14).

and urgings of this One leads to gradual conformity to this One. As disciples grow more conformable to the Spirit, the more resilient and compelling is their witness to this One's splendor. These represent many of the aspects of the sanctifying work of the Spirit today, the "other Paraclete" who does not leave Jesus' disciples orphaned.

The authority of Scripture

A number of important features of the canonical heritage could be highlighted for consideration in what follows. The sacraments, the episcopacy, creedal materials—these and others could be surveyed for expressing further the logic of the Spirit's mediation in and through created reality. This chapter will circumscribe the range of its purview to one such means of grace that is important to all Christians in varying ways; this resource is Holy Scripture. The Bible is particularly pertinent to this chapter's concerns since all Christians find it to be a fitting and exquisite expression of God's self-disclosure and so self-revelation to humankind. We have already noted in this book how Scripture provides pneumatology with a number of the most basic and fundamental tags and codings for its shape and form. To put it simply, the language of the Spirit is grounded and encased in the language of Scripture. Scripture shows its preeminence by shaping the church's speech, including its Spirit-speech. As such, Scripture is the church's authoritative text.

If one were to press a believer as to why the Bible is so important to the Christian life and faith, any number of particular descriptors might be proffered. One such descriptor—and for many the most important or pivotal of the possibilities available—would be that Scripture is "inspired." This language is picked up in large part because of the wording one finds in the first part of 2 Timothy 3:16, "All scripture is inspired by God." The Greek word translated as "inspired" can be rendered etymologically as "God-breathed" since it has the roots of the words "God" and "Spirit" (*theopneustos*). For many Christians, they would say that the Bible is authoritative, reliable for matters of faith, and true in its message because it is inspired or "God-breathed."[10]

---

[10]See Robert W. Wall's development of this notion in his commentary on *1 & 2 Timothy and Titus* (Grand Rapids, MI: Eerdmans, 2012), pp. 274–8.

The difficulty with this kind of formulation is that it can be taken to suggest that inspiration is a property of the biblical text, and if this is the case, then Scripture is by default isolated and maybe even marginalized from any number of its vitalizing factors and features.[11] For instance, if inspiration is a property of the biblical text, then one would be inclined to think that the property was registered at the time of the text's composition. Perhaps the biblical writers were "inspired" as they put word to parchment, and in doing so, their words retain the resonance of that dynamic of inspiration. As such, inspiration becomes part of the historical process of the text's coming to be so that particular historical-critical matters increase in importance, including authorship, place of composition, linguistic analysis, and so on.[12] As a result, the text's inspiration, similarly to its meaning within such a construct, would necessarily be a matter of author-centric concern. All of this would contribute to the reduction of the Bible's inspiration as largely a matter of historical inquiry and reconstruction. The text is inspired because it was written by inspired authors at a given time and place. One need only recognize this "property" so as to value and adhere to Scripture's authority.

Such moves have sundry hermeneutical implications. For instance, the depiction of "inspiration" as a property of a text feeds into the approach that the text's revelatory and sacred effects are simply there to be mined by any reasonable and open observer. A "common-sense" rationalism may come to exercise its influence in such (oftentimes apologetic) narrations so that it is understood that the Bible can be perceived as eloquent, literarily beautiful, and inspired all at the same time by those willing to exercise the human faculties necessary for such a recognition. Under this depiction, the

---

[11]Stephen Fowl states the concern here with an economy of expression: "Rather than making an assertion about a property of the text, however, Christians should best understand claims about scripture's authority as establishing and governing certain networks of relationships" (*Engaging Scripture* [Eugene, OR: Wipf and Stock, 2008], p. 3). Part of these relationships includes for me the relationship of the Spirit to the phenomenon that is Sacred Word.

[12]No wonder, then, that many in this camp would resort to speaking of the preeminence of the "original autographs" since by definition inspiration is understood as happening at this point and in no later process of the text's coming to be (including the varied and so "unreliable" processes of editing, copying, and transmission).

Bible's inspiration is embedded in the text, and so it is just a matter of convincing people to see the reality that already is there.

Why would approaches such as these be difficult? In short, the depiction of inspiration as a property of the biblical text results in the domestication of Scripture by bridling it largely to the historical process, and as such, this tethering leads to the domestication of the Spirit's said role in both the Bible's formulation and contemporary appropriation. These possibilities have taken effect among some communions in large part because of a variety of philosophical and hermeneutical reductions registered in full with the dawning of the modern era. They sometimes are a direct result of thinking of the Bible as an epistemological foundation of the Cartesian variety, a move that is sometimes at play when people advocate the *sola Scriptura* principle of scholastic Protestantism for the sake of grounding and specifying particular proposals in theological endeavoring. The assumed reliability of such a foundation is nothing short of a theological trump card par excellence.

An expansive pneumatology of Scripture

There is no need to dispute the role of the Spirit in the authoring of biblical texts. Although one may disagree strongly with a number of the philosophical and hermeneutical assumptions at play in some of these depictions, the general tenor of the impulse rings true: The Spirit was actively involved in bringing to be the texts that would make up the biblical canon. What would certainly be worrisome on this score would be the diminution of the Spirit's role to only this particular understanding of inspiration—as if the Spirit were only considerable as a feature of Scripture's coming to be in the historical process. If this is the case in a particular formulation of a theology of Scripture, then the account is startlingly impoverished from a pneumatological point of view.

What is needed on this score is nothing short of a generous and expansive account of the Spirit's role in Scripture's performances and appropriations today in the economy of sanctification.[13] To

---

[13]A work that extends this thematic compellingly is John Webster, *Holy Scripture* (Cambridge: Cambridge University Press, 2003).

put the matter suggestively: *Holy Scripture is a pneumatological phenomenon in all its many theologically relevant dimensions.* Certainly, one can say that the Spirit was involved at the point of composition, but this would represent only one aspect of its Spirit-constituted identity. One also has to account, for example, for the process of canonization. There were a number of possible texts that could have made it into the biblical canon. That some of these did while others did not is nothing short of the Spirit's moving through individuals, congregations, and councils to shape a "set-apart" or sanctified canon. Furthermore, the processes of copying and transmission need not be relegated to a "naturalized" process simply because it yields different results on the basis of the textual evidence available at any given time and place. Textual criticism, as for all forms of biblical criticism that are employed by students and scholars with the understanding that they are dealing with a sanctified text, should be understood within the Spirit's enabling and ongoing work of making this text the textual means of grace that it is. Finally, the point of proclamation and reception ought to be understood pneumatologically as well. The proclamation of Holy Writ is not simply the communication of words but the presentation of the gospel, which in turn beckons and challenges hearers as it is proclaimed. These many dimensions (composition, canonization, transmission, and proclamation) are noteworthy for any narration of how Scripture is "breathed out" by God to hearers and readers.

The reception and appropriation of this word must also be understood in a Spirit-related way, for the hearing and reading of Scripture *as* Sacred Writ can only be done on the basis of another work of the Holy Spirit, namely, illumination. The reception of Holy Writ is just as important to frame pneumatologically as is its delivery. As John Calvin noted, "The same Spirit . . . who has spoken through the mouths of the prophets must penetrate into our hearts to persuade us that they faithfully proclaimed what had been divinely commanded."[14] In fact, when many entertain the pneumatological dimensions of Scripture, the matter is usually ordered within a dynamic of two bookends: inspiration and illumination.[15] To

---

[14]John Calvin, *Institutes of the Christian Religion*, John T. McNeill (ed.), 2 vols (Philadelphia, PA: Westminster, 1960), p. 79.
[15]For a more extensive account of illumination, see John Webster, *The Domain of the Word* (London: T & T Clark, 2012), chapter 3.

expand on the latter matter, if readers come to the Bible with the
end of seeking the face of God, then undoubtedly they need God's
capacitation and guidance to do so. Certainly, God's self-disclosure
is crucial in this process, but the preparation and sanctification of
the intellect is a matter of relevant concern as well. The Spirit not
only brings forth a sanctified text that has been set apart for human
flourishing, but the Spirit also works through human intelligence and
perception to set apart faculties for the reception and recognition of
life-giving Spirit-happenings.

Finally, mention should also be made that these many points
associated with a pneumatology of Scripture operate out of an
implicit notion of divine providence: The Spirit has been working
all along in the production, transference, communication, and
reception of Holy Word. Like all means of grace or constituents
of the church's canonical heritage, the human dimension is not
neglected or obliterated in light of such providential work of the
Spirit; however, a thoroughgoing naturalized process would not be
a fitting characterization of such a dynamic. Rather, the Spirit works
through historical conditionedness and contextual particularity to
deliver and make operative within the church a text that can be a
means of grace for the church's healing.

With all of this variability understood to be conceptually
permissible in the construction of a pneumatology of Scripture, one
may wonder if Scripture is an unsettled category, one that is too
malleable or too conditioned by factors that could vary exceedingly
depending on particular circumstances. For instance, Scripture's
"truth claims" may be perceived to be complicated with mounting
manuscript evidence, or different readers may render the meaning
of biblical texts in exceedingly different ways. For some, these
possibilities in turn may be taken to be threats to the coherence and
so intellectual viability of a text understood to be an instrument
of the Trinity's self-presentation. In answer to these concerns, one
need only look at various features of Scripture's constitution and
character to show its *already* contestable status as a certain kind
of epistemological foundation. For instance, a vast segment of the
world's Christians includes the Apocrypha in their canon, and the
ordering of the books of the biblical canon can vary depending on the
Christian tradition in question. Additionally, the early church used
and cited the Septuagint translation of the Old Testament whereas
most today employ the Masoretic text. When different translations

are thrown into the mix of the Bible's reception, different renderings inevitably ensue, and these could have significant implications, both textual *and* theological. Just this sampling of the diversity and judgment-based features of the Bible's form and usage suggests that Scripture cannot be the kind of epistemological foundation that many wish it to be for the sake of doctrinal judgments and the formulation of the Christian life generally. And yet not simply in spite of this diversity but through it, the Spirit employs this text to form and shape disciples of the risen One.

To summarize and conclude this discussion of Scripture as exemplifying the Spirit's work of sanctification through the created realm: Can the Spirit be present and active in the midst of the "messiness" associated with a textual means of grace such as Holy Scripture? The answer entertained in this set of proposals is a resounding yes. However, for this judgment to be coherent, it requires some kind of alignment to another conceptual infrastructure besides modernist accounts of epistemology and hermeneutics that would promote Scripture's stability as a kind of foundation upon which an entire system of belief could be built. One key for such an alternative proposal would reside in the second half of the verse already cited for Scripture's inspiration, 2 Timothy 3:16, and the implications further found in the seventeenth verse, "All scripture is inspired by God *and is useful for teaching, for reproof, for correction, and for training in righteousness, so that everyone who belongs to God may be proficient, equipped for every good work*" (emphasis added). The alternative here would be to begin with Scripture's "usefulness" in the processes of discipleship, which would include the many activities outlined in verse 16. The end or goal is briefly alluded to in verses 15 and 17: instruction/wisdom, proficiency, being equipped. To expand on this last point, one can say that Scripture's identity and usefulness are tied to its performances and appropriations, ones that ultimately have as their goal or telos mature Christian faith. In this sense, Scripture's ontology is directly tied to its teleology.[16] The category of Scripture is infused and substantiated by the roles it plays within the economy of sanctification. If Scripture's raison

---

[16]I owe much of these insights of Scripture's usefulness to my colleague Robert W. Wall, who has repeatedly worked through these themes and with whom I have collaborated on a number of projects that elaborates them. See our forthcoming *The Marks of Scripture*, which is set to be published through Baker Academic.

d'etre is to build up a decisive and full-orbed Christian existence, then its authority and conceptualization should be substantiated accordingly. As noted above, a theme like Scripture's inspiration is not so much a property of the biblical text as it is a pneumatological function of that text in the collective history and life of a worshiping community who seeks to be conformed to the God they confess and worship.

Again, such a take on Scripture's authority may seem counterintuitive and possibly even dangerously unstable, but these matters are considerable as risks or threats only on the basis of certain formulations and conceptual apparatuses. If one begins with the premise that it is quite natural and fitting for the Spirit to work in and through the created realm, then that work can certainly involve the healing and emboldening of creatures through the means that the Spirit "sets apart" for holy ends and infuses with holy splendor. Such is the economy of sanctification: The Spirit works through people, events, and things to bring about the restoration of the created realm so that it may in turn participate in newer and ever-deeper ways in the holy life of God. Whether the relevant matters include creeds, hymns, prayer, or even Scripture, the Spirit is expansively and surprisingly at work *for* the world by operating *within* its aspects, conditions, and limits.

6

Receiving the Spirit

Spirit-Baptism and subsequence

*"Now he said this about the Spirit, which believers
in him were to receive;
for as yet there was no Spirit, because Jesus was
not yet glorified"*

JOHN 7:39

*"When he had said this, he breathed on them
and said to them,
'Receive the Holy Spirit'"*

JOHN 20:22

As noted earlier in this study, the language of "Spirit-baptism" is a tag or coding that is derivable from the NT.[1] Its most pronounced location is within the testimony of John the Baptist, one that is

---

[1] I use the language of "Spirit-baptism" or "baptism in the Spirit" for the sake of convenience with the full recognition that only the verb form "to baptize" (and not the noun form of "baptism") is associated with the Spirit in the seven, biblically relevant examples.

preserved in all four gospels (see Matt 3:11; Mark 1:8; Luke 3:16; John 1:33). In the Baptist's preaching, John's baptism is distinguished from Spirit-baptism, which would be dispensed by the One who was to come. This message represents a fusing of a number of themes. First, the Spirit being poured out was a common phrasing from the OT that suggested the age to come, as one can see with the prophecy of Joel 2. Typically, this pouring out of God's Spirit is understood to be undertaken by none other than God. Second, the expectation of a messianic figure being anointed by God's Spirit is also relatively common fare within Israel's scriptures. We have already drawn attention to both Isaiah 11 and 61 as passages in which a messianic figure was anticipated who would be empowered or anointed by God's Spirit. And yet, as James D. G. Dunn has noted, "There was no expectation of a messianic figure *bestowing* the Spirit in pre-Christian Judaism."[2] This observation shows quite pointedly just how distinct was the Baptist's message, leading Dunn to speculate that "the expectation of an eschatological redeemer himself 'baptizing' in Spirit was *the Baptist's own coinage.*"[3]

As important and distinct as John the Baptist's message was across the gospel traditions, one is also startled to find how such a prominent notion as "Spirit-baptism" early on in the NT was largely ignored and not more extensively taken up both in the outworking of the gospel traditions and all that would follow canonically in the NT literature. Certainly, the Book of Acts is important here since Jesus himself uses the tag in his post-resurrection appearances (1:5) and it is later picked up by Peter while referencing the Baptist's message when making his report to the Jerusalem church (11:16). In both cases—the first with anticipation and the latter looking back—Spirit-baptism is correlated with the happenings on the Day of Pentecost.[4] Yet these passages—the Baptist's four-gospel accounts and the two passages from Acts—as well as a Pauline reference

---

[2]James D. G. Dunn, "Towards the Spirit of Christ," in Michael Welker (ed.), *The Work of the Spirit* (Grand Rapids, MI: Eerdmans, 2006), p. 7 (emphasis added).

[3]Dunn, "Towards the Spirit of Christ," p. 9 (emphasis in original).

[4]Interestingly, Acts 2 does not explicitly make this connection; rather, Luke uses the language of "filling" (v.4) and depicts Peter as citing Joel 2 in terms of a "pouring out" as well as referencing the "promise" of the Spirit. The closest to such a coordination is Acts 2:38, where Peter remarks to the crowds: "Repent, and be baptized every one of you in the name of Jesus Christ so that your sins may be forgiven; and you will receive the gift of the Holy Spirit."

(1 Cor 12:13) form the entire gamut of exemplars of Spirit-baptism language in the NT. Therefore, it is perplexing that the Baptist's message, one which identified Jesus primarily as the Spirit-baptizer, should not be more pronounced in the rest of the NT. Little wonder, then, why the language has traditionally not been prominently registered in Christian consciousness.

Matters on this score have changed recently with the rise of the Pentecostal and charismatic movements across the globe. This "third stream" of Christianity is often credited with certain important instances of Christianity's renewal and growth across the planet. These movements often take the accounts of Acts in particular as paradigmatic for Christian existence, and in doing so, these groups make much use of the theological significance of the book as a whole but especially Acts 2. The Day of Pentecost represents for them a rupture in which OT expectations are fulfilled and NT developments (particularly what Jesus proclaimed and embodied in his own life, death, and resurrection) are significantly extended. This importance surrounding Acts 2, which is grounded not only in its own details but its localization within larger readings of God's providential and eschatological purposes, invests the language of Spirit-baptism with a degree of theological normativity. If Acts 2 is the fulfillment of God's purposes in Christ as proclaimed by the Baptist and anticipated by the OT, then Spirit-baptism can be understood as a significant way for describing some sense of Christian existence. These are some of the claims inherent to the message of Pentecostal and charismatic forms of Christianity, and their presence and advocacy have raised the stakes as to what this language of Spirit-baptism actually means.

With the questioning of this language, one can also see concomitant effects on a host of other, specifically pneumatological, issues. Of particular importance would be the shape and character both of the Christian church (including its narrations of practices such as the sacraments) and the Christian life (including its possibilities and forms). The language raises anew what kind of religion Christianity ultimately was in these early accounts and in turn what it could or maybe even should be in the present. To use Weberian language, was the early church a "charismatic community" that only later was "institutionalized" by growing forms of organizational and hierarchical structure? This line of questioning, although repeatedly pursued by scholars who concentrate particularly in early church history and Christian origins, has received additional attention in light of the rise of these modern-day movements. The Christian life too requires reconsideration in light of these kinds of Spirit-inquiries. Given the early biblical materials—which would include Acts but also the life, testimony, and operating assumptions detectable in figures such as Paul—one is burdened to ask: Is Christian existence and identity fundamentally or at least in some significant sense "charismatic" (as that term is typically understood)? Again, the language of Spirit-baptism increases the pressure surrounding such concerns. As Lesslie Newbigin remarked some time ago about the varieties of approaches to this notion: When Paul asked the Ephesians if they had received the Holy Spirit when they believed (Acts 19:2), probably something other than right teaching or proper ecclesial order was at stake.[5] Instances such as these have compelled Dunn to posit that quite possibly, "Christianity began as an enthusiastic sect."[6] If this reading has some merit, then it raises anew a number of considerations, including the question of the meaning and general associations with which Spirit-baptism is to be freighted in contemporary pneumatological discussions.

What follows is a general survey of three prominent alternatives for narrating and employing the tag "Spirit-baptism" within Christianity. Each option is instantiated and legitimated within larger ecclesial forms and theological constructs, so a resolution or synthesis is simply not possible at the dogmatic level. Nevertheless, given that these views rely on broader features of an explicitly Christian heritage, perhaps some headway can be made simply in terms of reframing the matters at hand. At least, that is the hope retained to some degree in the concluding section of the chapter.

Alternatives

Sacramental view

As noted, "Spirit-baptism" as a coding derivable from the Bible is not that pronounced in Scripture. However, there are specific cases

---

[5]Lesslie Newbigin, *The Household of God: Lectures on the Nature of the Church* (New York: Friendship Press, 1954), p. 104.
[6]Dunn, "The Work of the Spirit," p. 23.

in which a generic reference to "baptism" and reception of the Spirit play specific roles, and so the question arises: When Scripture simply speaks of "baptism," what precisely is meant? It appears that Jesus' disciples baptized people similarly to John (see John 4:1 where a comparison is drawn), but as the gospels suggest early on, Jesus is distinctly anticipated as the "Spirit-baptizer" and his baptism is distinguished from John's. Furthermore, is John's baptism a baptism of salvation or simply of anticipation? The instances of this language are undeniably ambiguous. For instance, take the passage from Mark's longer ending: "The one who believes and is baptized will be saved" (Mark 16:16). What does "being baptized" mean here? Or consider another example: Jesus at one point remarks: "I have a baptism with which to be baptized, and what stress I am under until it is completed" (Luke 12:50). In this case, Jesus was already baptized by the Baptist, but he goes on to speak of requiring another baptism, which appears to be in reference to his passion. In this case, "being baptized" apparently is a coding for the trials, suffering, and death associated with his crucifixion. Reception of the Spirit is a similarly challenging matter. Toward the end of John's gospel, Jesus breathes on the disciples and says, "Receive the Holy Spirit" (John 20:22). And yet at the end of Luke's gospel, Jesus tells the disciples that he is sending them the promise of the Father; therefore they are to wait in the city until they have been "clothed with power from on high" (Luke 24:49), a theme which—as we have already noted—is picked up in the first chapter of Acts. When do the disciples receive the Spirit, and can this moment—whichever it is—be counted as their Spirit-baptism?

Given this ambiguity as well as other important factors, some Christians have gone on to coordinate or conjoin water-baptism and Spirit-baptism this side of Jesus' work, in large part because of Jesus' own example. Recall that Jesus underwent John's baptism—which was essentially one of repentance—in order to fulfill all righteousness (Matt 3:15). And yet at that time, a series of additional phenomena occurred, particularly the descent of the Spirit in the form of a dove, as noted by all three of the synoptic gospels (Matt 3:16; Mark 1:10; Luke 3:22). The phrasing of the fourth gospel is also relevant here, for in the words of the Baptist: "I saw the Spirit descending from heaven like a dove, and it remained on him. I myself did not know him, but the one who sent me to baptize with water said to me, 'He on whom you see the Spirit descend and remain is the one who baptizes with the Holy Spirit'" (John 1:32–33).

The practice of water-baptism continued among Christians even after the onset of Jesus' ministry. Jesus himself commanded the disciples to baptize all nations (Matt 28:19) and they apparently did so in similar ways to John (as is the case with Philip and the Ethiopian eunuch; see Acts 8:36), but obviously their situation was also different from John's, particularly as they baptized after Jesus' resurrection and Pentecost. People who read these accounts may be inclined to conflate water and Spirit-baptism, but other cases draw a significant distinction between them. For instance, prior to Philip's encounter with the eunuch in Acts 8, Peter and John are said to travel to Samaria when they in turn find a group who had been baptized in the name of Jesus but who—we are told—had not yet received the Holy Spirit; therefore, Peter and John laid hands on them, and these believers are subsequently described as having received the Spirit (Acts 8:14–17). The pattern of coordination yet distinction is further mentioned in relation to Cornelius' household (Acts 10:44–48): The Spirit fell upon them, and they were in turn subsequently baptized in the name of Jesus Christ.

The most prominent traditions to advocate a coordinated approach would be the oldest ones, Roman Catholicism and Eastern Orthodoxy. This particular framing relates to sacramental matters, and of course, each of these traditions has its distinct sacramental understandings and practices. In terms of Roman Catholicism,[7] its *Catechism* makes explicit the role of pneumatological speech-forms within baptism itself: "This sacrament [of baptism] is also called '*the washing of regeneration and renewal by the Holy Spirit*,' for it signifies and actually brings about the birth of water and the

---

[7] In the following, the work of Kilian McDonnell and George T. Montague will be used to exemplify a dominant strand of Roman Catholic tradition, but they themselves recognize that another broad view is available, one that understands baptism in the Spirit as a special grace "unrelated to any immediate sacramental context" and taking as its cue certain passages from Thomas Aquinas (*Christian Initiation and Baptism in the Holy Spirit*, 2nd revised edition [Collegeville, PA: Liturgical Press, 1994], p. 93). They note Francis Sullivan as an exemplar of this perspective. Sullivan's views are more nuanced than this characterization allows, and his perspective is quite amenable to broad features inherent to both the "sacramentalist" and "Pentecostal" perspectives elaborated herein; see Francis A. Sullivan, *Charism and Charismatic Renewal* (Ann Arbor, MI: Servant Books, 1982), chapter 5.

Spirit without which no one 'can enter the kingdom of God.'"[8] This conjoining takes form through the prayer of epiclesis in which the Spirit is invoked so that the Spirit "may be sent upon the water, so that those who will be baptized in it may be 'born of water and the Spirit.'"[9] With these factors in mind, Kilian McDonnell and George Montague can say, "In the synoptics, Jesus' being anointed with the Holy Spirit from the moment of his baptism sets the pattern for Christian initiation, which is essentially a 'baptism in the Holy Spirit.'"[10]

Throughout their study, McDonnell and Montague note that a number of models or paradigms for Christian baptism have been used throughout Christianity; these would include: (1) Jesus' own baptism, (2) his death and resurrection, and (3) Pentecost. In their estimation, to this list *cannot* be added John's baptism, for early in their work, they emphatically claim that "the water-baptism by John, which many, if not all, of the disciples had received, was not Christian baptism."[11] Even though John administered Jesus' baptism, "the uniqueness of the event was proclaimed by divine intervention and the gift of the Spirit anointing Jesus with power."[12] With this depiction, a privileging of Jesus' baptism for an understanding of Christian baptism is on display, which is not unusual since shifts of emphasis have occurred among the options listed above. From their perspective, these authors believe that Jesus' baptism as a model for Christian baptism historically diminished in certain sectors for a host of important reasons; nevertheless, they wish to reclaim its primacy in continuity with how they read some of the earliest Christian sources on the topic. Jesus' baptism is the model for

---

[8]*Catechism of the Catholic Church* (New York, Image Doubleday, 1995) §1215 (p. 342, emphasis original).

[9]*Catechism of the Catholic Church*, §1238 (p. 348).

[10]McDonnell and Montague, *Christian Initiation and Baptism in the Holy Spirit*, p. 350.

[11]McDonnell and Montague, *Christian Initiation and Baptism in the Holy Spirit*, p. 27.

[12]McDonnell and Montague, *Christian Initiation and Baptism in the Holy Spirit*, p. 28. They further add, "The gift of the Spirit upon Jesus, though occasioned by John's baptism, was not mediated by it. On the contrary, the Spirit not only anointed Jesus but in some way effected a sanctifying of the baptismal water through him. Far from the water sanctifying Jesus, Jesus sanctified the water for all subsequent baptisms in his name" (p. 28).

Christian initiation because in their eyes his baptism in the Jordan *was* his baptism in the Spirit.[13]

Christians are to follow suit: They are to be baptized in water *and* to receive the gift of the Spirit (the latter sometimes symbolized through the laying on of hands). It is not that both baptism in water and the gift of the Spirit are one and the same, but one is naturally tied to the other as witnessed in Jesus' example. In living into this model, Christians become members of Christ's body through the act of God available in the rites of initiation (baptism, confirmation, and Eucharist). At play in this outworking are the primordial act of God and human responsiveness/participation. As such, Spirit-baptism in this model is a public event within the domain of the church's liturgy rather than a moment or experience within an individual's personal life of piety. Just as all witnessed Jesus' baptism in the Holy Spirit, so too are others to experience Spirit-baptism publically before an onlooking world.

Particularly impressive about the proposals by McDonnell and Montague regarding Christian initiation as "baptism in the Holy Spirit" is that a full bevy of charisms are said to be available to believers on the basis of the work of the Spirit at the point people are welcomed into the faith. These charisms vary significantly from the more institutional to the more charismatic variety, yet McDonnell and Montague allow for the full gamut of possibilities (as enumerated in such lists as Romans 12, 1 Corinthians 12, and Galatians 5) within the particular ethos of Roman Catholic life. Within this fellowship, the gifts—including the so-called charismatic ones—are not exceptional per se as they are "normal." As these authors relate, "In some way, the charisms, including the prophetic ones, structure the church," that is, they help facilitate a fellowship that can organize itself in a mutually benefiting form of complementarity so that the faithful's life together is built up and strengthened. They continue, "If the church is built upon the apostles and the prophets (Eph 2:20), the charisms are in some way essential."[14] Without going to the extreme of overly emphasizing

[13]McDonnell and Montague, *Christian Initiation and Baptism in the Holy Spirit*, p. 340.
[14]McDonnell and Montague, *Christian Initiation and Baptism in the Holy Spirit*, p. 368.

them, one can say that "the charisms are . . . a premise to the day-to-day life of the normal healthy communion."[15]

These authors recognize that with time the expectation and manifestation of these charisms have possibly waned among the sacramental traditions. Especially when infant baptism is involved, it may not always be clear how and why people do not go on to live into and demonstrate the charisms they are granted at the time of their baptism. This is a problem these authors rightfully acknowledge as worrisome. Part of the call inherent to their volume is to reclaim the expectation of the charisms for church life, leading them to say in the case of the Christian initiation of adults that the act "should . . . follow the pattern of the New Testament and create the *expectation* not only of an *experience* of the Spirit but of some *charismatic* manifestation as evidence of the reception of the Holy Spirit."[16] For those baptized as infants, the accompanying expectation of some kind of manifestation in the future should also be at play; with time as they gain knowledge and experience, those baptized as infants are to live into and actualize the grace already bestowed to them at their baptism.

To conclude, we have taken McDonnell and Montague as representative of the sacramentalist view of Spirit-baptism, one which is coordinated with water-baptism so that these work together within the broader processes of Christian initiation. This depiction is inherently dynamic in that human realization is possible and needed so that the community of faith flowers and blooms into its call. Certain Catholic charismatics have been able to appropriate this view since it depicts the charismatic and institutional features of church life in complementary and mutually glossing ways, but again, this view is aimed at the whole of the church and its liturgical life and not simply its charismatic streams.

Evangelical view

Another approach to the one surveyed above is oftentimes associated in the present academic climate with one figure and his influential

---

[15]McDonnell and Montague, *Christian Initiation and Baptism in the Holy Spirit*, p. 371.

[16]McDonnell and Montague, *Christian Initiation and Baptism in the Holy Spirit*, p. 90.

text: James D. G. Dunn's *Baptism in the Holy Spirit*. Others would also fit into this broad camp since this particular perspective works well within broad Protestant evangelical commitments, particularly ones that do not assume a sacramental apparatus in the same way as the model surveyed above does.[17] Of course, even in these evangelical camps the trope of Spirit baptism is not used in the same way across their many forms, but Dunn's work has generated significant influence in the conversations on these matters over the last few decades, and for this reason, his work will be highlighted as representative in what follows.

Straight on, Dunn claims that his goals in the work are "to show that for the writers of the NT the baptism in or gift of the Spirit was part of the event (or process) of becoming a Christian" so "that it was the chief element in conversion-initiation . . . only those who had thus received the Spirit could be called Christians."[18] Furthermore, Dunn adds his belief that "the reception of the Spirit was a very definite and often dramatic *experience*, the decisive and climactic experience in conversion-initiation, to which the Christian was usually recalled when reminded of the beginning of his Christian faith and experience."[19]

In this sense, Dunn is self-consciously trying to offer a middle-option of sorts between the other alternatives surveyed here: On the one hand, Dunn believes that Spirit-baptism is tied to Christian initiation, but he does not see this initiatory process exclusively in sacramental terms, for he believes that from Acts forward one could make the argument that "water-baptism is clearly distinct from and even antithetical to Spirit-baptism."[20] Dunn does not believe that water-baptism should be confused with Spirit-baptism (a gesture he

---

[17]See for instance John R. W. Stott, *Baptism and Fullness: The Work of the Holy Spirit Today* (Downers Grove, IL: InterVarsity, 1979). Stott conflates a number of tropes, as is indicative in the following quote that elaborates the happenings early in Acts: "We could sum it up by saying that these penitent believers received the *gift* of the Spirit which God had *promised* before the Day of Pentecost, and were thus *baptized* with the Spirit whom God *poured out* on the Day of Pentecost" (p. 25, emphasis original). As his title suggests, however, Stott does draw a distinction between baptism and fullness, the latter marking a dynamic state that must be tended to through the ongoing practices of Christian discipleship.
[18]James D. G. Dunn, *Baptism in the Holy Spirit* (Philadelphia, PA: Westminster Press, 1970), p. 4.
[19]Dunn, *Baptism in the Holy Spirit*, p. 4 (emphasis original).
[20]Dunn, *Baptism in the Holy Spirit*, p. 5.

associates—rightfully or wrongfully—with the sacramentalist point of view), and in light of this concern, one senses the importance of his emphasis on "conversion" within this dynamic. On the other hand, Dunn holds that the Pentecostal separation between initiation-conversion and Spirit-baptism "is wholly unjustified" given the NT evidence.[21] The point is illustrated in the other word of his construction ("initiation"), for he believes that "the high point in conversion-initiation is the gift of the Spirit, and the beginning of the Christian life is to be reckoned from the experience of Spirit-baptism."[22] Apparently, he very much appreciates the possibility of Spirit-baptism being a crisis-oriented event or development—a dramatic happening so to speak. But he is quite adamant to counter what can be called the Pentecostal logic of subsequence.

Clearly, certain biblical passages would fit Dunn's reading more so than others. For instance, what would he do with the Johannine witness, one that can contribute to the bifurcation of Spirit-experiences through its emphasis on Jesus breathing on the disciples in a concrete way prior to the happenings on the Day of Pentecost? The canonical voice of John and this concern in particular are considered in the fourth part of his volume. Initially, Dunn wishes to be careful in conflating witnesses together, in this case the Johannine with the Lukan. Since John does not record a Pentecost event, assuming its role in a cross-testamental timeline may be difficult, at least on first blush. Dunn is committed to looking—at least initially—at the function of events within their own canonical units, so in this sense the inbreathing of the Spirit in John 20 should be seen on its own terms before the effort is made to reconcile it with Acts 2.

A second way of dealing with this concern on Dunn's terms is to consider the experience of the disciples as non-repetitive history. In other words, the experience of salvation for the disciples is not so much a model for subsequent believers but rather a unique phenomenon given that their experience spans a number of unrepeatable events that are landmarks within salvation history. Case in point: Dunn reads the ascension of Jesus as marking the end of the old covenant and the bestowal of the Spirit after the

---

[21]Dunn, *Baptism in the Holy Spirit*, p. 4.
[22]Dunn, *Baptism in the Holy Spirit*, p. 4.

ascension as the beginning of the new. Given that the disciples'
experience spans both, in their unique case they had a different
"conversion-initiation" dynamic than those who would follow
their lead as Christ-followers. In this sense, John 20 may have been
a kind of "Pentecost for the disciples" within the Johannine witness
that functions similarly to the Acts 2 narrative within the Lukan
corpus. Dunn admits that this particular reading of the Johannine
literature is not the easiest, but he finds it viable, both on its own
terms and in light of the other relevant biblical materials.

Part of the reason for Dunn's influence has been that
Pentecostal and charismatic scholars have taken his proposals as
a direct challenge to their own; therefore, an entire generation of
Pentecostals and charismatics in the academy has focused their
energies and endeavoring so as to rebut the central claims Dunn
makes in *Baptism in the Holy Spirit*. Some of the most concerted
and influential efforts have been those of Roger Stronstad[23] and
Robert Menzies.[24] Both of these scholars see in Dunn a privileging
of a Pauline model for Spirit-baptism; in their view, Paul's view of
the role of the Spirit in the Christian life is largely related to coming
to faith, and it is this paradigm, they charge, which Dunn goes on
to generalize to the whole of the NT witness.[25] They counter this
Pauline view directly with a Lukan view, and in the case of the latter,
they find it irrefutable that Luke depicts a logic of subsequence,
which will be the focus of what follows.

Pentecostal view

The previous two proposals had in common the idea that Spirit-
baptism was tied to Christian initiation. A third pattern offers a

---

[23]Roger Stronstad, *The Charismatic Theology of St. Luke* (Peabody, MA:
Hendrickson, 1984).

[24]Robert Menzies, *Empowered for Witness* (Sheffield: Sheffield Academic Press,
1994).

[25]For his part, Dunn is aware of this critique, and he would charge that the
Pentecostals have engaged in a reduction of their own, one in which their portrayal
of Luke's accounts of Spirit-baptism and the Spirit's working has little to do with
Christian initiation-conversion. For more on Dunn's reaction to the charge, see
James D. G. Dunn, *The Christ and the Spirit*, vol. 2 (Grand Rapids, MI: Eerdmans,
1998), chapter 17.

different approach. Its adherents hold that subsequent to the experience of Christian initiation there is another detectable moment, one in which a person experiences an affective alteration and empowering outpouring of God's Spirit. Whereas the previous patterns draw a coordinated approach between Christian initiation and Spirit-baptism, this last group significantly distinguishes them so that Christians, having already come to faith, are encouraged to press into another modality of Christian existence. Part of the rationale for this posture is (again) said to be scriptural precedent: The disciples were followers of Jesus and were even breathed upon by Jesus according to John's gospel, but they nevertheless had to wait in Jerusalem for the promise of the Father. This promise was realized over the span of days, and their spiritual autobiographies would no doubt be inflected by some sense of subsequence: they were Jesus' disciples, yet they were instructed by Jesus: "You will receive power when the Holy Spirit has come upon you; and you will be my witnesses in Jerusalem, in all Judea and Samaria, and to the ends of the earth" (Acts 1:8). Therefore, tied to Christianity's early self-understanding in terms of experience and proclamation was this sense of the need for "something more" in terms of power and signs. For most Pentecostals[26] and many charismatics,[27] the idea of this subsequent experience has been encapsulated through the tag of "Spirit-baptism."

Various revivalist, renewalist, and pietist groups throughout Christian history have advocated the need for a subsequent experience to Christian initiation in the Christian walk. This additional encounter was often denominated in different ways, but the language of Spirit-baptism, given what was detected to be the patterns of Luke's accounts especially, has been a strong

---

[26]There are notable exceptions within the Pentecostal camp on this score, perhaps the most famous example being Gordon Fee; see his *Gospel and Spirit* (Peabody, MA: Hendrickson, 1991), particularly chapter 7.

[27]The label "charismatics" here refers to those who experienced renewal in the 1950s and 1960s in many mainline churches particularly in the United States. Usually, they stayed within their church traditions (thereby not forming their own denominations) and often they took up the logic of subsequence inherent to Pentecostalism. For these reasons, they are being grouped in this chapter within the "Pentecostal" alternative. For a broad survey of possibilities, see H. I. Lederle, *Treasures Old and New: Interpretation of "Spirit-Baptism" in the Charismatic Renewal Movement* (Peabody, MA: Hendrickson, 1988).

possibility in several cases. Consider, for example, the happenings
of early Methodism: Throughout his ministry, John Wesley spoke
of the need for sanctification and Christian perfection in a context
(primarily eighteenth-century England) that had experienced
Christian lethargy, and yet his appointed successor, John Fletcher,
went on to use the language of "baptism in the Holy Spirit" to
speak of this sanctifying call, a move that Wesley himself did not
denounce.[28] As movements of renewal extended from the eighteenth
to the nineteenth centuries, the Holiness Movement picked up on
both the need for a subsequent experience to Christian initiation
as well as the occasional coding of such an experience in terms of
"baptism in the Spirit."[29] In a move similar to Fletcher's, those of the
Methodist variety were calling for an experience of sanctification
that some also called Spirit-baptism. Furthermore, others within
the Holiness Camp (for instance, the Keswick and "Higher Life"
movements) maintained that an experience was needed in which
people were empowered for Christian service along the lines of the
Lukan narratives. With these rumblings in previous centuries, the
stage was set for the Pentecostal movement of the twentieth century
to use the language of "Spirit-baptism" in order to denominate an
experience that was deemed subsequent to Christian initiation.

 Given these historical underpinnings, the early Pentecostal
movement of the American variety—which is often deemed "classical
Pentecostalism"—was largely birthed out of the nineteenth-century
Holiness Movement. This interconnectivity can be seen in the life
of one of the figureheads of the movement, Charles Fox Parham.[30]
Largely working in the American Midwest, Parham was a faith-
healer and preacher who early in his ministry was associated with
the Methodist church. When Parham went on to be ecclesially

---

[28]An ongoing scholarly debate exists on this point, led in part by Donald Dayton and
Laurence Wood; for a summary of the interchanges, see Amos Yong, "Response #2,"
in Christian T. Collins Winn (ed.), *From the Margins: A Celebration of the Theological
Work of Donald W. Dayton* (Eugene, OR: Pickwick, 2007), pp. 179–90.

[29]For an early essay that documents this transition historically, see Donald Dayton,
"From 'Christian Perfection' to the 'Baptism of the Holy Ghost,'" in Vinson Synan
(ed.), *Aspects of Pentecostal-Charismatic Origins* (Plainfield, NJ: Logos, 1975),
pp. 39–54.

[30]An indispensable work for understanding Parham's legacy is James R. Goff,
Jr., *Fields White Unto Harvest: Charles F. Parham and the Missionary Origins of
Pentecostalism* (Fayetteville: University of Arkansas, 1988).

independent, he traveled throughout the United States to learn from other major Holiness leaders of the time. One such trip proved to be decisive; he visited Maine in the summer of 1900 to learn from Frank W. Sandford in a community the latter had established. After his time in Maine, Parham was compelled to return to his native Kansas in October of that year so as to set up a similar training school to prepare missionaries for worldwide outreach; he named this school Bethel Bible College. A couple of months later in December, Parham challenged his students to look for the "Bible evidence" for Holy Spirit baptism, for by that time Parham had become convinced that such an empowering experience would usher in a global revival. He left for a few days on a preaching trip, and when he returned, he reported that the students had come to a consensus, which was that the one prevalent Bible evidence for Spirit-baptism was speaking in tongues. The group proceeded to "seek the blessing," and famously, an aspiring missionary by the name of Agnes Ozman reportedly spoke in tongues on January 1, 1901.

In light of the historical materials available, one can see that Parham already had basic features of the "tongues-evidence" understanding established in his mind prior to his students' conclusion. One can further note that much of this line of thought was developed during his time at Sandford's school, where Parham actually witnessed tongues-speech. It is telling, after all, that he returned from Shiloh, Maine with the intent of establishing a *missionary* training school, for tongues-speech had a pivotal role in Parham's understanding of this end-times worldwide revival. In short, the general understanding coming out of these happenings was that Spirit-baptism was an experience subsequent to conversion for the empowerment of believers to engage in worldwide evangelism in a period deemed as penultimate to Jesus' second coming. The Bible evidence of tongues proved helpful here since for Parham, the tongues in question were *xenolalia*—foreign human languages per the Acts 2 pattern. That the evidence for Spirit-baptism was *xenolalia* was crucial for Parham's vision since the experience would allow people to become instant missionaries for the global revival to be ushered in during the "latter days." Within the revivalist context of worship, people simply had to discern which foreign tongue they were speaking when they were baptized in the Spirit so that they could know where God was calling them to serve.

Eventually, Parham fell out of favor with the emerging Pentecostal establishment, yet Parham's logic was largely retained by classical Pentecostal denominations. These groups continued to advocate tongues as the initial, physical evidence of Spirit-baptism, although they modified Parham's views by substituting *glossolalia* (unknown tongues) for *xenolalia*. This move in addition to the gradual waning of Pentecostalism's early missionary impulse contributed to the morphing of Spirit-baptism from being an experience of empowerment for end-times evangelism to one that edified the individual believer. With these shifts, American classical Pentecostalism in particular (which is the background for many denominational forms that have a global presence) stumbled upon what was claimed by many as the doctrinal distinctive of the movement: the experience of Spirit-baptism, subsequent to conversion, as evidenced by the initial, physical evidence of tongues or *glossolalia*. Many Pentecostals and charismatics throughout the world have not adhered to what can be termed "initial-evidence thinking" when accounting for their views on Spirit-baptism, but they alongside their American, denominational counterparts have typically promoted the logic of subsequence, that Spirit-baptism is best understood as an experience of empowerment and capacitation subsequent to Christian conversion or initiation.

Orienting proposals

As noted above, both what we are calling the "sacramental" perspective (as embodied by the work of McDonnell and Montague) and the "evangelical" alternative (as represented by Dunn) share the view that Spirit-baptism is best thought of in relation to people coming to the Christian faith. Of course, each envisions that process differently, but they hold the view that the Christian life does not consist of distinguishable steps as the Pentecostal alternative apparently does with its logic of subsequence. With the latter group, Christian initiation or conversion is one matter whereas Spirit-baptism is another, not simply at the conceptual register but at the experiential as well. Where does this leave us in terms of making sense of the coding "Spirit-baptism"? Is there a way forward in the midst of these competing visions?

To answer these questions, one has to be forthcoming about expectations and possibilities. For instance, a theme sounded throughout this book is how indeterminate Spirit-talk is in Scripture. One such instance is precisely related to those passages that speak of being baptized in the Holy Spirit. Not only are these passages relatively few within the biblical canon, but their reference and meaning are unclear as well. We have already noted how, despite the Baptist's imagery for Jesus as the "Spirit-baptizer," one is startled to find how largely ignored and underdeveloped the theme is throughout the NT. Given this degree of indeterminacy and underdevelopment, one naturally finds specification for the notion on the basis of other theological—and so ecclesial—arrangements. Therefore, one's view of Spirit-baptism is largely formed by the particular communion of which one is a member. If one is a Pentecostal Christian, the trope "Spirit-baptism" will simply mean something very different from what it would mean in other ecclesial forms. The assumption that everybody will come to a consensus or workable agreement simply through thoroughgoing exegetical endeavoring is misguided, for it does not recognize that at the heart of these disagreements are not simply exegetical differences but also (and more fundamentally) communal commitments and practices. For the "sacramentalist," the entire sacramental structure of Christian initiation substantiates the trope; for the "evangelical," specific commitments surrounding Christian conversion are at play; and for the "Pentecostal," the trope's exegetical elaborations are largely funded by a deemed normative experience available in the context of revivalist worship. Given that these are the matrices in which "Spirit-baptism" is lodged, little by way of securing consensus for the trope's meaning can be on the horizon.

Part of the difficulty inherent to these discussions and treatments has to do with the project overall. Essentially, efforts to make sense of "Spirit-baptism" are working within the larger task of conceptually securing and elaborating the Christian life. If this is the larger agenda, then of course the matter is tenuous from the start given the daunting character of the assignment (a theme which has been sounded already in this book). How does one go about conceptually narrating a life—not just the Christian life but any life for that matter? When people speak of others or themselves, they usually begin in terms of details related to origins (birthplace, date of birth, family of origin, and so on) and move to consider "landmark" moments such as school transitions, significant relationships, major crises and triumphs, and so forth. As helpful as those narrations are, however, human lives are not reducible to them. Human selves are so much more than their biographies— even their autobiographies—can relate. Something analogous is at play in efforts to communicate and relate the Christian life, either at the particular or general level. People come to the Christian faith in a number of ways, and these are embedded within a host of particular details. This complexity is primarily due to the creaturely dimensions of human existence: The Christian life is lived across time and in the midst of a number of details and circumstances; for these reasons, it plays out in a number of ways.

All the traditions above will generally recognize that *the Holy Spirit is involved from the beginnings of the Christian life.* To lead the life of a Christian is to be prompted, aided, and guided by the presence and work of the Holy Spirit. Those beginnings may take different forms (including ecclesial ones), but the Spirit's role is crucial in whatever one wishes to say about the very core and heart of what it means to lead the life of a Christian. This point may be occluded from time to time in the heat of discussion and debate, in part because different tropes and linguistic phrasings may be privileged to secure contested points. But whatever the specified terminology and sacramental activity associated with the beginnings of the Christian life, the Holy Spirit is God's presence manifest and graciously at work in the redemption, healing, and sanctification of God's creatures.

The challenge that the "Pentecostal" alternative poses, one that many forms of the other two alternatives have considered extensively and critically, is the matter deemed "subsequence." Are there multiple experiences of the Spirit, and so marks of the Christian life, that are normative for all Christians to have? Anecdotally, one hears a number of possibilities, including those that would offer either a resounding "yes" or "no." One of the difficulties with the "Pentecostal" perspective is the tacit assumption that experiences with God are "out there" to be had by Christians as long as the conditions are right (and plenty of debate exists as to what those conditions are and how they can be pursued and secured). Functionally, a two-level understanding of the Spirit's work not only creates a two-tiered approach to Christian experience but also more worrisomely a "two-class" valuation of Christian identity—for instance, those who have the subsequent experience of Spirit-baptism and those who do not. Obviously, this construal is ready-made for use in efforts that work against Christian unity and charity.

At the same time, those under the "Pentecostal" umbrella can propagate a serious call to their Christian counterparts. This call does not simply have to do with living out Christian existence in accordance with expectations garnered from the first-century church (so that people come to believe that what happened "then" as reported in the Book of Acts can happen "now"). The call goes deeper still through the implicit recognition that the Christian life involves depth-registers. Because it is about a certain way of living, Christian existence has to be accounted for in a manner that seriously considers not simply the possibility but the need for growth and the striving after maturity. As noted above, "Pentecostal" approaches to recognizing these depth-registers have often been propagated with particular claims regarding religious experience, ones that indelibly have the stamp of modernity upon them. According to this view, Christians at the individual level are "to have" particular landmark moments that they could point to and say (in the case of our present example), "At that moment I was baptized in the Spirit." This approach to religious experience has significant drawbacks in our current, consumerist culture, for it easily devolves into the commodification of Christian spirituality and so the Christian life generally. As difficult as this model is, however, part of the warrants for its ongoing appeal and propagation is that it recognizes Christian identity as not simply a status but a mode of existence or a way of "being-in-the-world" that is dynamic, inflected, and shaped by the very process of living. For those of the "Pentecostal" persuasion, the logic of subsequence helps account for this basic concern. Whatever one's views on the logic of subsequence and the assumptions regarding religious experience that it carries and the propriety in using the "Spirit-baptism" tag to account for it, I would venture to say that another basic claim that most Christians can agree on is that *the Christian life necessarily involves maturation, and this growth, too, involves the presence and work of the Holy Spirit.*

When individuals or communities go on to demarcate stages in growth or development in the Christian life, problems naturally arise. People may resist being categorized within a schematization of "stages of faith" for similar reasons they would in terms of developmental models such as Erikson's: The process can just come off as too confining and too driven by a master-narrative that is itself tentative and carries with it a number of contestable assumptions. But Christians have been wrestling with accounting for depth-registers or depth-dimensions to their common life for some time now. Biblical authors themselves struggle with the theme: Paul marks a distinction between those who "drink milk" and those who "eat solid food" (1 Cor 3:2) and the writer of First John uses a tripartite ordering of children, young people, and adults (2:12–14). The early church also faced this challenge in a variety of ways; one of the most long-standing efforts in this regard has been the rise and perpetuation of monasticism.

I wish to stress one broad theme tied to this notion of growth. On first blush, this notion may appear little related to the topic of Spirit-baptism and the logic of subsequence overall. And yet, the current discussions on Spirit-baptism are significantly at a standstill because of their present shape. Those formulations that have attempted to broaden the trope's applicability carry with them the most promise,[31] yet challenges continue. The indeterminacy of "Spirit-baptism" as a trope, competing ecclesial framings, and exegetical and theological formulations following therefrom—these are all constitutive of a significantly entrenched and stifling state of affairs. An altogether different account may be necessary in order to advance the discussion, one that can be attentive to Clark Pinnock's point that "the rhythm of actualization [of the Spirit's power in a believer] varies from person to person."[32]

When the topic of growth in the spiritual life is broached, one possible term worth considering is *epiktasis*, the noun form of the word used by Paul in Philippians 3:13, which can be translated in its verbal form as "straining forward." This notion relates to the self's perpetual ascent in and toward God; it is beckoned in service of elaborating the mystical dimensions of the Christian life, for it helps cast that life as one driven primarily by its grounding, sustenance,

[31]These would include from the Pentecostal side of the discussion Frank Macchia, *Baptized in the Spirit: A Global Pentecostal Theology* (Grand Rapids, MI: Zondervan, 2006) and Amos Yong, *The Spirit Poured Out on All Flesh: Pentecostalism and the Possibility of Global Theology* (Grand Rapids, MI: Baker Academic, 2005), particularly chapter 2.
[32]Clark H. Pinnock, *Flame of Love: A Theology of the Holy Spirit* (Downers Grove, IL: InterVarsity, 1996), p. 169.

and end in the triune God of Christian confession. Paul captures the dynamic beautifully: "Now the Lord is the Spirit, and where the Spirit of the Lord is, there is freedom. And all of us, with unveiled faces, seeing the glory of the Lord as though reflected in a mirror, are being transformed into the same image from one degree of glory to another; for this comes from the Lord, the Spirit" (2 Cor 3:17–18). Crucial in the Apostle's framing is the sense of being "on the way": The past is important, but the thrust of the momentum is aimed toward the future, the end. As such, this proposal is inherently and thoroughly eschatological since God is portrayed as the telos of Christian existence. If God is the goal of such a life, then there are infinite riches to experience, fathom, and embody.

One of the difficulties in framing the Christian life in terms of rites of initiation, an experience of conversion, or crisis moments that are chronologically separable is that there is simply so much that remains ahead or before the Christian community both experientially and practically. Christians live on the basis of not simply what has already happened but also in terms of what is to come. And as for what has happened, the Christian life is simply not reducible to certain landmark moments in one's past, however important those are. For these many reasons, the idea of *epiktasis* reminds formulators of the Christian life that Christian existence is an endless enchantment with the Trinity. Wonder and amazement are not simply fleeting emotions but abiding dispositions that mark the whole of the Christian life because these are ordered and directed to God. If the Christian life is truly *pneumatikos* ("spiritual"), then it can mean nothing less than what Rowan Williams suggests in terms of the vision of the Christian life held by Gregory of Nyssa: "If the Christian life is a journey into God, it is a journey into infinity . . . faith is *always*, not only in this life, a longing and trust directed away from itself towards an object to which it will never be adequate, which it will never comprehend. God is what we have not yet understood, the sign of a strange and unpredictable future."[33] *Epiktasis* helps keep at the forefront of Christian reflection the commitment that the Christian life is about desiring and becoming conformable and enchanted with the Father, Son, and Holy Spirit. In specific terms related to the Spirit, *epiktasis* accounts for the way

---

[33]Rowan Williams, *The Wound of Knowledge: Christian Spirituality from the New Testament to Saint John of the Cross* (Lanham, MD: Cowley, 1990), pp. 65–6.

the Spirit can work in the mundane and the everyday features of our lives so as to kindle a desire for a God who has no end. As important as landmark moments are, they are best situated within a broader dynamic, one that accounts for the Spirit's presence within the rhythms of existence and the Spirit's work of awakening and fanning anticipation, desire, and expectation.

Conclusion

By way of concluding the major themes of this chapter: Spirit-baptism is a trope that has received considerable attention over the last few decades particularly because of its weighted role in Pentecostal and charismatic circles. Different church traditions have gone about narrating its significance in varied ways in large part because the trope itself is largely underdeveloped in Scripture. Three broad alternatives were considered in this chapter; they have been labeled for convenience as the "sacramental," "evangelical," and "Pentecostal" views. All three make important contributions to the discussion, yet at the same time they can be reductive since their employment is directed with the aim to conceptualize a certain kind of life. For this reason, this chapter surveyed what are largely recalcitrant approaches, but it ended with the hope that discussions related to the Christian life can be reframed so that growing vitality and an abiding desire for God can be prioritized in such discussions.

7

Guided by the Spirit

Discernment

"When the Spirit of truth comes, [this One] will guide you into all the truth"

JOHN 16:13

"But the Advocate, the Holy Spirit, whom the Father will send in my name, will teach you everything, and remind you of all that I have said to you"

JOHN 14:26

The Seventh Assembly of the World Council of Churches met in Canberra, Australia, during February 7–20, 1991 around the theme "Come, Holy Spirit—Renew the Whole Creation." It was the first WCC Assembly explicitly ordered around the motif of the Holy Spirit, but of course, pneumatology, at least implicitly, is always an important factor for any ecumenical gathering. The Nicene confession that the church is one, holy, catholic, and apostolic is both a pneumatological possibility as well as an ecclesial vocation. Commendable of this particular meeting was that it was organized also in the form of a prayer, a version of the "Veni" already surveyed in this text. A meeting of this kind is quite the event, given the variety of cultures and points of view. The Official Report of the Assembly highlighted this diversity in a positive and celebratory way: "We rejoice in the diversity of cultures, races and traditions represented at the assembly, and we give thanks to God for the many expressions of the Christian faith and for the growing sense of unity amidst this diversity."[1]

The question of discerning the Spirit was a prevalent one at this gathering. This Assembly's deliberations and formulations indicated a strong openness to various forms of Spirit-talk, an openness stemming from the commitment that the Spirit is at work among all peoples and blows wherever it wills. This approach, however, is difficult to sustain, and the Assembly found this out firsthand. The issue came to a head with the presentation of Chung Hyun Kyung, then of the Presbyterian Church in South Korea. In her opening remarks, she called upon the spirits of a number of people and things, including biblical victims, modern-day liberators, the Amazon forest, and so on. She did so largely because of resources she drew from her own Korean context. Especially prominent in her presentation was the concept of *Han*. At one point, she remarked, "I come from Korea, the land of spirits full of *Han*. *Han* is anger. *Han* is resentment. *Han* is bitterness. *Han* is grief. *Han* is broken-heartedness and the raw energy for struggle for liberation. In my tradition people who were killed or died unjustly became wandering spirits, the *Han*-ridden spirits."[2] Incorporation of cultural idioms is always important and to some degree unavoidable in theological reflection; nevertheless, one imagines that part of the controversy with Chung's remarks had to do with how she drew those connections. At a later point, she added, "Therefore the living people's responsibility is to listen to the voices of the *Han*-ridden spirits and to participate in the spirits' work of making right whatever is wrong. These *Han*-ridden spirits in our people's history have been agents through whom the Holy Spirit has spoken her compassion and wisdom for life. Without hearing the cries of these spirits we cannot hear the voice of the Holy Spirit."[3] Chung went on to say: "For us, [these *Han*-ridden spirits] are the icons of the Holy Spirit who became tangible

[1]Michael Kinnamon (ed.), *Signs of the Spirit: Official Report of the Seventh Assembly of the World Council of Churches* (Grand Rapids, MI: Eerdmans, 1991), p. 1.
[2]Kinnamon, *Signs of the Spirit*, p. 39.
[3]Kinnamon, *Signs of the Spirit*, p. 39.

and visible to us. Because of them we can feel, touch and taste the concrete bodily historical presence of the Holy Spirit in our midst."[4] These are simply the opening remarks of Chung's presentation, one that involved a number of cries against armament, ecological destruction, and greedy materialism as well as calls for genuine repentance and an increased sense of the interconnectivity between all life forms and the earth.

There are many positive features to be drawn from Chung's presentation, yet some concerns present themselves as well, ones directly related to the theme of discernment of the Spirit's work in cultural forms. For instance, how is it that *Han*-ridden spirits become the conduits of the voice of the Holy Spirit? What does the implied "spirit-realm" in her remarks look like and how is it constituted? Later in her speech, Chung drew another connection, one in which she remarked that the image of the Holy Spirit that came to her was in the form of *Kwan In*, who is "venerated as the goddess of compassion and wisdom by East Asian women's popular religiosity."[5] Does the Spirit of Jesus take on images from other deities, and if so, how does one demarcate any kind of tension or difference between the two?

Unsurprisingly, many found her remarks as demonstrating a kind of syncretism. Consider the probative response by the Orthodox delegation to the Assembly:

> It is with alarm that the Orthodox have heard some presentations on the theme of this assembly. With reference to the theme of the assembly, the Orthodox still await the final texts. However, they observe that some people tend to affirm with very great ease the presence of the Holy Spirit in many movements and developments without discernment. The Orthodox wish to stress the factor of sin and error which exists in every human action, and separate the Holy Spirit from these. We must guard against a tendency to substitute a "private" spirit, the spirit of the world or other spirits for the Holy Spirit who proceeds from the Father and rests on the Son. Our tradition is rich in respect for local and national cultures, but we find it impossible to invoke the spirits of "earth, air, water and sea creatures." Pneumatology is inseparable from

---

[4]Kinnamon, *Signs of the Spirit*, p. 39.
[5]Kinnamon, *Signs of the Spirit*, p. 46.

Christology or from the doctrine of the Holy Trinity confessed
by the church on the basis of divine revelation.[6]

If the Spirit is at work at all times and all places among all
peoples, then how does one know what is truly "of the Spirit"
from what is not? If the Spirit's work is always mediated, are some
mechanisms of mediation more suitable than others, and how
would one know the difference? In other words, the question of
discerning the Spirit's presence and work is often front and center
in pneumatological discussions since all too often people cite the
Spirit's activity quite easily: Appeals to the Spirit are readily found
as a way of securing support for claims or agendas that at the end
of day may be mutually incompatible. On the one hand, Chung's
concerns raise an important point, namely that the Spirit can work
through Korean cultural forms just as prominently and effectively
as European or Mediterranean ones. At the same time, the concerns
of the Orthodox delegation also ring true: At some point and in
some way, a difference has to be conceptually available, for the
integrity of Spirit-talk demands that it cannot simply be whatever is
"already there" as detected by cultural observers and brokers.

One of the underlying commitments of this chapter is that
discernment is no easy process. Some may wish for a simple solution
to the perplexity, one derived from a moment of Spirit-induced
clarity or a reasonable process of weighing inspired materials with
other things. This expectation, however, is highly idealized, for it
operates not out of a fundamental faith-conditioned awareness per
se (in which doubt and the "conviction of things unseen" play a
role) but rather a kind of generalized epistemic certainty-rubric. As
Levison reminds us, illumination and hard work go hand in hand;[7]
one without the other is an impoverishment, not simply in terms
of results but of process, method, and (most crucially) formation
as well.

This chapter will not offer a formulaic approach to discernment,
which will be understood here not simply with respect to "discerning
spirits" but much more directly in terms of the way one comes

---

[6]Kinnamon, *Signs of the Spirit*, p. 281.
[7]Such is a running theme in *Inspired: The Holy Spirit and the Mind of Faith* (Grand
Rapids, MI: Eerdmans, 2013).

to know and live into what the Spirit's presence and work might indicate to the worshiping faithful at a given time and place.[8] At play is a breadth of consideration one finds available in 1 Corinthians 2:14–15, in which those who are "spiritual" are able to discern "all things." Of course, with discernment typically comes the question of criteria, which is a complicating theme to say the least. As appealing as the *Didache* was in its detailed criteria for identifying false prophets, one is struck by how this process necessarily entails more than simply assessing a person's character, which may or may not involve if a person stays longer than three days or asks for money.[9] Furthermore, the practical challenge that different church traditions approach discernment in widely varying ways means that a formula to settle all disagreements on this score is simply impossible. What this chapter will do is to probe deeper into both the complications and potential shape of discernment. A particular model from one church tradition will be assessed, and larger concerns for the Christian life will be broached. With this last point, this chapter is a fitting conclusion to this book, for pneumatological concerns are bereft of their true shape when depicted apart from the challenge of Christian existence. All theology—and especially pneumatology—has to be lived in the midst of the complicating pressures and demands of the everyday.

Discernment and method

The question of discernment runs head-on alongside the question of theological methodology. Simply put, when people raise the concern of identifying the Spirit's presence and work, they are in turn asking the question of where to look, what counts as evidence, and what the goals of such endeavoring are. In other words, discernment requires

---

[8]In the more specific sense of the prior consideration, Amos Yong has repeatedly been a helpful voice. See his early work *Discerning the Spirit(s): A Pentecostal-Charismatic Contribution to Christian Theology of Religions* (Sheffield: Sheffield Academic Press, 2000) as well as his later *Beyond the Impasse: Toward a Pneumatological Theology of Religions* (Grand Rapids, MI: Baker Academic, 2003).

[9]*Didache*, 11.5–6 as found in Michael W. Holmes, *The Apostolic Fathers in English*, 3rd edition (Grand Rapids, MI: Baker Academic, 2006), p. 169.

some primary account of what are the sources, norms, and ends of the theological task.[10] Given that different theological outlooks and persuasions will value and frame each of these differently, varying outcomes are necessarily the result.

In terms of sources, different traditions and theological orientations will differ considerably on this very basic question: *Where is the Spirit at work?* Some, like Chung, will look to cultural expressions and believe to see the Spirit of God working through these on the basis of an underlying commitment to the Spirit's interpenetration of the entire creaturely realm. Given that the world is because God brings it to be and given that all of humanity reflects the image of God and not simply self-professed Christians, touch points necessarily exist between the confession of the Holy Spirit and popular religious expressions of varying contexts. Therefore, these thinkers may be inclined to ask what the Spirit of God is already doing amid popular religious forms. Still others may say they appeal to the Bible as their primary source for theological construction, and in so doing, they ineluctably promote a particular hermeneutical orientation. Within this view, the Bible is the eternal Word of God writ clearly for those who are willing to attend to its witness and precepts. Potentially others may rely on a received tradition or teaching office of that tradition, a magisterium. One senses such an approach in the Orthodox reaction to the Assembly, for the delegation appealed to a rich tradition's resources to substantiate their points (including the language of procession and the link between Christology and pneumatology). Cultural expressions, sacred texts, teaching traditions—these and many others often function as the sources by which theological constructs are rendered and so they represent an orienting baseline by which to engage in the discernment process.

Tied to sources is the notion of norms, which in our case would involve the question: *What is the Spirit's work?* Obviously, the category of norms suggests matters related to propriety, fittingness, and authority. Norms reckon with the idea of standards, of what "counts" or what one uses in order to evaluate and deem something un/viable or un/successful. Norms are tied to sources because

[10]I am indebted to John Webster for the economy of expression at this point. See his "Introduction" in John Webster, Kathryn Tanner, and Iain Torrance (eds), *The Oxford Handbook of Systematic Theology* (Oxford: Oxford University Press, 2007).

the latter have a way of framing and setting up the former. If a theological source is a teaching document or church posture on a matter, then a norm will go on to privilege features or marks of those sources in ways that determine larger features of communal life, including identity, polity, and so forth. If a source is a textual witness, then situating oneself within a particular reading of that source is crucial methodologically, theologically, and even politically. Each tradition and each theological outlook maintain an operative account of their ideal forms, processes, virtues, and outcomes. Tags often traffic to depict such specifications; examples include "love," "open-mindedness," "liberation," "justice," "orthodoxy," and even "the Bible." Behind these norms, however, are usually political and communal power arrangements and orders so that certain accounts and renderings simply fit and others do not on the basis of power brokers, authority figures, and political pressures. As much as some would wish to have norms be a neutral category in this regard, one cannot help but point out that norms work alongside partisan formations.

Finally, the question of ends is important because it drives the question of purpose, which according to this volume's thematic would be: *What is the Spirit ultimately trying to do?* Some perspectives may say that the Spirit is trying to bring about greater equality or freedom in the world. Others may stress the question of justice and suffering: the Spirit is on the side of the oppressed and therefore is at work to liberate them and in turn make the world more humane. Still others may say that the Spirit is working to convict the world of sin so that people come to know Christ as their Savior and Lord, with this recognition taking the form of a particular profession of faith. Of course, these ends or purposes need not be mutually exclusive, but their diversity point once again to larger matrices of signification and meaning-generation. The purpose-question is already largely settled by what one has gone on to conclude about where to look and what counts as normative for a community's self-understanding.

Therefore, on all three counts—sources, norms, and ends—one sees webs of interconnected concerns. At the least, their interstices form the following: expectation-sets ("What are we hoping to find and achieve?"), plausibility structures ("What is possible and impossible in such work?"), and conceptual and practical desiderata ("What counts as good and worthy to pursue?"). These many matters involve fundamental methodological concerns and determinations, ones that are simply too complex to consider here in all their dimensions, but when taken collectively, they point to the way and degree to which Christian theology is a significantly internally contested discipline. Furthermore, they point to how discernment is such a precarious, provisional, and challenging form of endeavoring.

A methodological test case

As a way of demonstrating some of the complexities associated with this topic, we will look to a particular construct that is often used in the process of discernment. Among many people, if anything is known of Wesleyan theology, it is the so-called Wesleyan Quadrilateral. There is some irony to this state of affairs since John Wesley never used the language of a "quadrilateral" nor applied all four of its deemed features in a systematic, organized way so that this in turn represents his contribution to theological methodology. The construct itself was coined in the late 1960s by Albert Outler,[11] the father of the modern turn to Wesleyan/Methodist studies within the theological academy. The Quadrilateral is essentially composed of four theological authorities—Scripture, tradition, reason, and experience. Scripture was assumed to be the Protestant Bible, and its preeminence is often tied to the statement Wesley made for himself—that he was a "man of one book." Tradition for Wesley had largely two aspects: the witness of the early church (particularly its pre-Nicene witnesses) as well as his Anglican heritage (throughout his life he was a member and churchman of the Church of England). Reason was largely viewed by Wesley as a cognitive capacity,

---

[11]The phrasing made its way to public consciousness via an interim report issued in 1970 to the General Conference of the United Methodist Church by a committee chaired by Outler. For a brief history and assessment of the Quadrilateral, see Ted Campbell, "The 'Wesleyan Quadrilateral' : The Story of a Modern Methodist Myth," in Thomas A. Langford (ed.), *Doctrine and Theology in The United Methodist Church* (Nashville, TN: Kingswood, 1991), chapter 11. For Outler's own warrants for the construct, see his "The Wesleyan Quadrilateral—In John Wesley" in the same collection (chapter 6).

a faculty of the mind for ordering and putting things together. And finally, experience was a running emphasis in Wesley in that he granted theological legitimacy to affective and transformative dimensions of the Christian life.[12] Some of the most prominent of Wesley's phrases would be related to this last category, including "the altogether Christian," "the new birth," "the circumcision of the heart," and the idea of "heart religion." One of Wesley's favorite verses for this last dynamic is Romans 8:16, "It is that very Spirit bearing witness with our spirit that we are children of God." For many years, scholars attributed this experiential importance within Wesley's perspective to a particular event in his own life: the "heart-warming" experience on Aldersgate Street, London in 1738.

Of these four, three were already in circulation as a set of theological sources in Wesley's day. Richard Hooker helped establish Scripture, tradition, and reason as resources for the Church of England as it came out of the Elizabethan Settlement of 1559. Outler took this Anglican heritage and added the notion of experience since it rang true for Wesley's ministry and the form of early Methodist life: As a revivalist movement within the Church of England in the eighteenth century, Methodism highlighted the role of pietistic experience with the explicit aim of cultivating renewal within the church. In trying to make sense of Wesley's thought-processes, particularly as they related to controversial and difficult matters (which were always a significant feature of Methodist life), Outler noticed particular arrangements and formations of these at pivotal junctures in Wesley's oeuvre. For instance, to drive a point home or to make a significant line of argument ring true, Wesley was often prone to appeal to Scripture, church tradition, reason, or experience (or a combination of these). Therefore, the Quadrilateral is a mechanism derived from the collective witness of Wesley's works that allows for some kind of methodological determination for those attempting to make sense of Wesley's thought in particular and Wesleyan theology in general. People outside of this tradition have also found it valuable so that in both cases, the Quadrilateral has often been pressed for service as a kind of discernment tool.

---

[12]Two works that illustrate features of each of the Quadrilateral's emphases is Donald Thorsen, *The Wesleyan Quadrilateral* (Grand Rapids, MI: Zondervan, 1990) and W. Stephen Gunter, Scott J. Jones, et. al., *Wesley and the Quadrilateral* (Nashville, TN: Abingdon Press, 1997).

One suspects that many have found the Wesleyan Quadrilateral helpful because of the way it can function as a mechanism to broaden horizons as to what constitutes theological authorities in constructive theological reflection. The granting of legitimacy to experience, for instance, may be helpful for those pietist traditions that may feel pressured at times to think that respectable theology only takes the form of drawn out, definitional declarations and formulas. Part of the appeal of the Quadrilateral may also be tied to its assumed simplicity, which could take the following form: If one tests an idea by looking at what Scripture, church tradition, reason, and experience say, then one can come to a fairly straightforward and viable conclusion as to what is a salutary course of action on the matter. In other words, the Quadrilateral is sometimes taken to be a discernment "assembly line," which can be put to use so as to process a concern or pressing matter in a way that yields a helpful, "finished" product.

One of the most outspoken critics of the Quadrilateral has been William Abraham, a scholar already highlighted in this book given his work with the "canonical theism" project. Speaking out of his own particular denominational context of The United Methodist Church, Abraham worries that the perpetuation of the Quadrilateral has serious consequences for a churchly condition in which "doctrinal amnesia" is at play. Abraham argues against the Quadrilateral's role in doctrinal matters by stating, "At its heart the quadrilateral involves a fatal running together of a reduced account of ecclesial canons with the norms of Enlightenment theories of knowledge."[13] Put "graphically" (and colorfully!), he believes the binding of these authorities is akin to a "hastily contrived shotgun wedding between scripture and tradition, the bride provided by the church, and reason and experience, the bridegroom, provided by the European Enlightenment."[14] Essentially, Abraham is worried with the way these authorities have been put together as representative of an epistemic instrument. And admittedly, he has a point. In both form and practice, the Quadrilateral simply cannot deliver the epistemic goods that so many seek it to do.

---

[13]William J. Abraham, *Waking from Doctrinal Amnesia: The Healing of Doctrine in The United Methodist Church* (Nashville, TN: Abingdon, 1995), p. 61.
[14]Abraham, *Waking from Doctrinal Amnesia*, p. 61.

Abraham's assessment rings true for a number of reasons. At a basic level, it is not clear how each one of these authorities is to be defined. We have already noted in this work how "Scripture" is not a self-evident category since many variables are at work in its particular instantiations, including translations, church communions, hermeneutical orientations, and so on. In terms of "tradition," Wesley favored the ante-Nicene fathers as well as his own Anglican heritage. Of course, within each of these broad streams there is tremendous diversity. Furthermore, different Christian communities are going to appeal to different traditions and figures as matters play out and concerns present themselves. There is something to be said for something like a "Great Tradition" within Christianity, but for the kind of particularity that is often sought through the utilization of the Quadrilateral, the differences do matter and inevitably determine variant outcomes.

This diversity points to a larger concern. Whatever one makes of "Scripture" and "tradition," they are essentially of a different order than "reason" and "experience." As noted earlier in this study, the first two are best understood as "canons" or "means of grace" to aid in the church's sanctification; the latter, on the other hand, are "concepts of justification or rationality" best suited within the technical philosophical field of epistemology.[15] This categorical conflation and subsequent application yield a process that is highly unworkable, for the fruit of this endeavoring conceals more than it illuminates. For this reason, Abraham concludes that "the quadrilateral, even in its most carefully stated form, does not show how we are to resolve potential conflicts between the various sources,"[16] and as such, I would add: It cannot definitively help with the process of discernment.

Some have found broad warrants for the Quadrilateral at various points in Scripture, particularly Acts 15. In this Jerusalem Council, the nascent church was facing a significant crisis, that is, how to account for the swelling ranks of converted Gentiles within an originally Jewish movement. The prompting question was: Do Gentiles have to be circumcised (i.e. in a sense become good Jews)

---

[15]Abraham, *Waking from Doctrinal Amnesia*, p. 62. As noted earlier, this argument is sustained more broadly by Abraham in *Canon and Criterion in Christian Theology*.

[16]Abraham, *Waking from Doctrinal Amnesia*, p. 63.

in order to be saved (v. 1)? Eventually, the Council formulated a letter that contains the famous phrasing, "For it has seemed good to the Holy Spirit and to us to impose on you no further burden than these essentials" (v. 28). As indicated by this language, discernment of the Spirit's work was explicitly at play, and in looking at how the Council arrived at its judgments, one notices that they made reference both to the ancestors and the prophets, including Moses (Scripture and tradition); they also deliberated and discussed the situation (reason), and they went on to listen to the signs and wonders witnessed by Barnabas and Paul (experience). For many, then, the Quadrilateral in roughshod form can be detected in Acts 15; therefore, they conclude, it can serve as a model for discerning what the Spirit is saying and doing in the midst of troubling and confusing situations.

This rendering of Acts 15 so as to justify the Quadrilateral's ongoing relevance suffers from an anachronistic bent. Certainly, Acts 15 demonstrates how the church in a particular situation went about seeking and discerning God's will. As made obvious by the text, a number of factors went into this process—as they should have, given the severity of the matter at hand. Nevertheless, the consideration of Acts 15 as a "discernment template" is itself a gesture that betrays a number of assumptions, ones that also perpetuate (and plague) the ongoing application of the Quadrilateral itself. One such assumption is that discernment is essentially—to cite the language already at play in Abraham's reservations—a kind of "calculus," that is, a kind of mathematical logic or ordering based on a premised evidentialism. Simply put, some believe (and the use of the Quadrilateral only strengthens such a belief) that just as "two plus two equals four" one can also "add" and cull together what Scripture, tradition, reason, and experience say so that an obvious "solution" is yielded from such a process. This approach betrays a certain kind of rationality. To be sure, discernment does indeed operate out of a particular logic, but its form is not mathematical or instrumental, which seems to be the kind usually assumed in the Quadrilateral's usage.

A second, seriously damaging premise that builds on the first is the penchant toward abstraction and decontextualization with the Quadrilateral's use. In particular, if discernment is a certain kind of "calculus" (the first assumption), then the persons or community engaging in the discernment process can do so without accounting for their own embeddedness, and this is a problem because all of us bring bits and pieces of ourselves to such a process as this one. The ambiguity of each of the four constituents of the Quadrilateral only helps mask this form of abstraction, for distinct communities can go on to "pick and choose" within the particular offerings of the rubric what they find most favorable. In other words, the process is set up to yield predetermined outcomes. People will see and appropriate in the Quadrilateral what they are already inclined to see and do. To further complicate matters, given that such a process is described as "theological discernment," one could go on to "sanctify" and "spiritualize" any number of competing and contradicting outcomes by making the claim that the Spirit is involved when arriving at the aforementioned (and to some degree predetermined) conclusions. The claim "what the Spirit is saying to the churches is *this*" could be a veil for any number of agenda-laden proposals. It is no wonder why the "masters of suspicion" of the modern era were so keen to point out religious hypocrisy since so much of what comes out of theological endeavoring in the name of discernment can be portrayed as projectionist at its core.[17] From one angle of consideration, people believe what they want to believe, and they can theologically legitimize these choices by saying that they are prompted and spurred on by the Holy Spirit to do so.

Discernment?

If discernment is fraught with these many debilitating concerns, then what can one say about it? Is discernment ultimately an impossibility? At the end of the day, is it nothing but a "special-interest" activity that cannot escape its parochialism and partisanship? As daunting as they may first sound, one need not capitulate to such fatalistic and pessimistic conclusions. After all, every vantage point is offered from "somewhere," and as noted earlier in this book, the Spirit works

---

[17]In such cases, these critiques can be aids for the church's sanctification, an approach taken by Merold Westphal in *Suspicion and Faith: The Religious Uses of Modern Atheism* (New York: Fordham University Press, 1998); in other words, these claims need to be taken seriously by Christian communities since they may be true even if they are offered from outside the faith.

through these determinations and contingencies to accomplish the Spirit's purposes. The Spirit and particularity are not at odds with one another. Quite the contrary, the Spirit empowers the particular to stretch beyond its assumed limitations.

One way to make a certain kind of progress on these matters is to recall discernment's proper theo-logical character. What may be lost in the advocacy of a "discernment calculus" is the recognition that at play in discernment of the Spirit is in fact *the Spirit*, and such a process is necessarily of another order than one's run-of-the-mill rationality or epistemology. What is needed is something akin to what Amos Yong has called a "pneumatic imagination."[18]

The situation could be described in the following way: *To discern the Spirit, one needs capacitation by the Spirit.* At one level, such a claim sounds circular. Certainly, the Spirit is needed by way of the Spirit's self-presentation. But what about capacitation? This matter is much more challenging to narrate. Discernment—as with all other matters of the spiritual life—is self-involving. The difficulty, of course, is that many Christian traditions are at a loss or awkwardly inclined in terms of how to secure this point conceptually and linguistically. The worries are often located on a spectrum that aims to avoid two extremes: determinism on one end and a kind of Pelagianism on the other. Christians are often perplexed because they wish to give glory and praise to God, yet they also want to make sure that human activity and striving are not neglected but cast in proper perspective.

Once again, pneumatology's indeterminate nature may be helpful in this case, for this quality creates space for human agency and striving. The Spirit's work and human striving need not be cast as competing on the same agential level. Quite the contrary, their domains are necessarily distinct and each is of a different order. And yet, their intermingling at the very core of the calling to be "Spirit-bearers"—which would include walking according to the Spirit, living in the Spirit, in short being people of the Spirit— contributes to a condition of "synergistic indeterminacy" as one speaks of Christian living. The phrase "synergistic indeterminacy" is intended to point to how the Holy Spirit and the human spirit are involved in Christian flourishing, a dynamic prompted by Paul's

---

[18]See his *Spirit-Word-Community: Theological Hermeneutics in Trinitarian Perspective* (Eugene, OR: Wipf and Stock, 2002).

own phrasing: "For if you live according to the flesh, you will die; but if by the Spirit you put to death the deeds of the body, you will live" (Rom 8:13). In this dynamic, the Spirit is involved to be sure ("by the Spirit"), yet humans actively participate as well (they "put to death") as they are further drawn into God's very own life. Given the prompts of Scripture, this dynamic can take shape both negatively and positively. On the negative side, there are several codings in the NT that speak of how human striving can go against and even stifle the work of the Spirit. These instances include blaspheming the Spirit (Matt 12:31–32), lying to the Spirit (Acts 5:3), resisting or opposing the Spirit (Acts 7:51), grieving the Spirit (Eph 4:30), quenching the Spirit (1 Thess 5:19–21), and insulting or outraging the Spirit (Heb 10:26–29). Whatever one may wish to say in support of safeguarding God's omnipotence or sovereignty, the implications of these passages suggest that God has created arrangements in which people can reject and work against God. On the positive side, Scripture lists a number of charisms that are oftentimes denominated differently. Typically, Christians speak of these varying taxonomies as Spirit-related; they may be spoken as gifts generally (Rom 12:6–8 and Eph 4:11) or particularly as gifts of the Spirit (1 Cor 12:4–11) as well as fruit of the Spirit (Gal 5:22–26). Within these positive lists, people sometimes try to go one step further and delineate particular logics pertaining to each. This strategy might be heuristically helpful, but, whatever one's opinion on such particular strategies, it does not take away from the point that the Spirit-imbued life is a Spirit-enabled and Spirit-capacitated one that requires on the human side a kind of involvement that has both passive (in terms of capacitation) and active dimensions (in terms of cultivation and realization).

I have elsewhere spoken of this synergistically indeterminate situation as one involving an "epicletic" form of existence.[19] This term speaks to the invocation of the Spirit during sacramental liturgical rhythms. The language of epiclesis helps secure the point that the Spirit is the One who is called upon by none other than the worshiping faithful. Both entities—the Spirit and the Spirit's worshipers—are involved in the proceedings of baptism, Eucharist, and other forms of worship. An "epicletic existence," therefore,

---

[19]See broadly Daniel Castelo, *Revisioning Pentecostal Ethics—The Epicletic Community* (Cleveland, TN: CPT Press, 2012).

speaks of a certain modality of being, one that is doxological to its very core. And precisely because it is a sacramental term, "epiclesis" resonates with larger concerns related to the theological task (and so of discernment as well). When Christians seek and speak of walking by and living in the Spirit, they do so under the doxological framing that living in a certain kind of Christ-normed way is the most fitting service and homage they can render. As doxological, this life is prompted, grounded, and finds its end in the triune God of Christian confession, and yet it has to be lived, embodied, and performed in a certain kind of way. It involves a specific kind of coinherence in which God and the church are intertwined in definitive ways.[20]

These are the "contextualizing" conditions, I would say, that are involved in the discernment process, and as such, they counter the tendencies toward decontextualization and abstraction one often finds in proposals related to such activity. If discernment is not a kind of "calculus" of instrumental logic undertaken by decontextualized selves, then it has to be a form of activity that is explicitly recognized and sought as vitalized by the Spirit's abiding and ongoing presence and work within sacramental time and space. Only "epicletic" selves can engage in faithful discernment of the Spirit since discernment is itself an "epicletic" form of endeavoring. Summarily stated, *discernment is a Spirit-dependent and Spirit-enabled kind of endeavoring undertaken within the modality of Christian worship.* Only this kind of modality will allow for: (1) the proper recognition of what kind of activity discernment actually is, (2) the fitting and necessary chastening of human intellection and activity before and in the Blessed Trinity within space and time, and (3) the general orientation that this work will serve to render glory to God through the restoration, transformation, and renewal of all things, including the community that is called and desirous to seek the face of God.

Given these conditions, what kind of outcomes can one expect? On the one hand, one need not give short shrift to a kind of

---

[20]Illustrative of this dynamic is the vine and branches imagery of John 15. The basic claim of verse 4 ("Abide in me as I abide in you") is further registered horticulturally in verse 5: "I am the vine, you are the branches. Those who abide in me and I in them bear much fruit, because apart from me you can do nothing." The interaction is dynamic since it involves ongoing sustenance, vitalization, and connectedness.

Spirit-enabled "empirical" capacitation. Christians throughout the ages have recognized this possibility through the language of the "spiritual senses." Although different accounts of these will stress varying themes, a galvanizing motif around the spiritual senses is that as one grows in conformity to Christ by the participation made available by the Spirit, different realities and dynamics present themselves to attentive believers. Over time, people learn to "see," "taste," "hear," and "feel" reality on different registers as a result of continually sitting at the feet of Jesus.[21] These kinds of considerations raise Christology to some criteriological degree, which is typically the case in Christian accounts of discernment. However, "Christ" is not some principle, proposition, or other kind of epistemic category. Both in his lifetime and in his present resurrected state and ascended location, "Christ" is a personal, Spirit-endowed entity who may or may not be appreciated for who he is when one encounters him. That some people then and now do or do not follow him because of what they think they witness when they behold him is broadly put quite determinedly a Spirit-infused dynamic. The prospect of something akin to a "Spirit-empiricism" helps illustrate that what Christians come to see, hear, taste, smell, and feel because of a Spirit-capacitation or Spirit-intensification is nothing short of a registering and reconfiguration of a kind of "tacit" God-knowledge that only the Spirit could occasion and only the human could imbibe.

This Spirit-capacitation and/or Spirit-intensification has to be sustained in the ways that it can from the human side of the dynamic. Time is involved alongside a kind of attentiveness and intentionality. The existentially epicletic dynamic of abiding and waiting—so beautifully rendered in the imagery of John 15—depicts discernment as a kind of responsive and formative activity. The kind of formation at play is not simply relatable in terms of becoming more and more like God in some abstract sense; it involves the increased capacity to "live into the story" of Christian identity in the midst of ever-pressing challenges and unexpected circumstances.

---

[21]Throughout the history of Christian reflection, different accounts of the spiritual senses have emerged from the time of Origen. For a helpful recent survey, see Paul L. Gavrilyuk and Sarah Coakley (eds), *The Spiritual Senses* (Cambridge: Cambridge University Press, 2012).

Various works by N. T. Wright,[22] Kevin Vanhoozer,[23] and Samuel Wells[24] have all shown this honed and developed ability to live more faithfully into the features of Christian existence. And precisely because these models concern themselves with living Christian existence in the particularities of the everyday, their vibrancy and effectiveness turn on the perduring influence and work of the Holy Spirit as a people obey the call of God to deny themselves, take up their cross, and follow Jesus.

Are these outcomes and expectations realistic? Are they even sufficient, especially when they are compared to the results that spring forth from instrumental modes of reasoning? Obviously, we all come to the task of discernment with a number of expectations of what should come out of such a process. We all have our accounts of what is authoritative within the theological task, including the sources, norms, and ends for such work. A pneumatological account of discernment, however, has to take a specific shape, one that reckons with the ways the Spirit works in and through the creation. Subtlety, fragility, provisionality—these are some of the marks of such activity. And also, there is the issue of formation. As startling as it is to claim, the writers of the *Didache* were on to something: Discernment involves the exercise and detection of character and virtue. It is not undertaken with unaided reason but within a pneumatological imagination or horizon, one that is attuned to the Spirit's work in the modality of Christian worship. A community can discern the ways of the Spirit as they desire and stay attuned to the Spirit in their everyday, worshipful lives. Another Johannine passage helps indicate what is at stake: "Anyone who resolves to do the will of God will know whether the teaching is from God" (John 7:17). Those who resolve and desire the will of God will in turn be capacitated and shaped by the Spirit to discern the ways of God.

---

[22]N. T. Wright, *The New Testament and the People of God* (Minneapolis: Fortress, 1992).

[23]Kevin Vanhoozer, *The Drama of Doctrine: A Canonical-Linguistic Approach to Christian Theology* (Louisville, KY: Westminster John Knox, 2005).

[24]Samuel Wells, *Improvisation* (Grand Rapids, MI: Brazos, 2004).

BIBLIOGRAPHY

Unless otherwise stated below in their respective versions and
   translations, sources from antiquity are taken from the *Ante-Nicene
   Fathers* (*ANF*) and the *Nicene and Post-Nicene Fathers, First* (*NPNF1*)
   and *Second Series* (*NPNF2*), all published by Hendrickson Press
   (1994).

Abraham, William J. *Waking from Doctrinal Amnesia: The Healing of
   Doctrine in The United Methodist Church*. Nashville, TN: Abingdon,
   1995.

—, *Canon and Criterion in Christian Theology*. Oxford: Oxford
   University Press, 1998.

Abraham, William J., Jason E. Vickers and Natalie B. Van Kirk (eds),
   Canonical Theism: A Proposal for Theology and the Church. Grand
   Rapids, MI: Eerdmans, 2008.

Athanasius, *On the Incarnation*, trans. A Religious of C.S.M.V.
   Crestwood, NY: St. Vladimir's Seminary Press, 2002.

Athanasius the Great and Didymus the Blind, *Works on the Spirit*,
   trans. Mark DelCogliano, Andrew Radde-Gallwitz, and Lewis Ayres.
   Yonkers: St. Vladimir's Seminary Press, 2011.

Augustine, *The Trinity*, trans. Edmund Hill, O. P. Brooklyn, NY: New City
   Press, 1991.

Ayres, Lewis, *Nicaea and Its Legacy: An Approach to Fourth-Century
   Trinitarian Theology*. Oxford: Oxford University Press, 2004.

Badcock, Gary D., *Light of Truth and Fire of Love: A Theology of the
   Holy Spirit*. Grand Rapids, MI: Eerdmans, 1997.

Basil the Great, *On the Holy Spirit*. Crestwood, NY: St. Vladimir's
   Seminary Press, 2001.

Boersma, Hans, *Heavenly Participation: The Weaving of a Sacramental
   Tapestry*. Grand Rapids, MI: Eerdmans, 2011.

Bonhoeffer, Dietrich, *Creation and Fall: A Theological Exposition of Genesis
   1–3*, trans. Douglas Stephen Bax. Minneapolis: Fortress Press, 1997.

Briggman, Anthony, *Irenaeus of Lyons and the Theology of the Holy
   Spirit*. Oxford: Oxford University Press, 2012.

Broderick, Robert C. (ed.), *The Catholic Encyclopedia*. Nashville,
   TN: Thomas Nelson, 1976.

Calvin, John, *Institutes of the Christian Religion*, John T. McNeill ed., 2 vols. Philadelphia, PA: Westminster, 1960.

Castelo, Daniel, (ed.), *Holiness as a Liberal Art*. Eugene, OR: Pickwick Publications, 2012.

—, "Holiness *Simpliciter*: A Wesleyan Engagement with John Webster's Trinitarian Dogmatics of Holiness," *Wesleyan Theological Journal* 47.2 (2012): 147–64.

—, *Revisioning Pentecostal Ethics—The Epicletic Community*. Cleveland, TN: CPT Press, 2012.

—, "The Spirit, Creaturehood and Sanctification: On Avoiding Theological Overcompensation," *International Journal of Systematic Theology* 16.2 (2014): 177–91.

Catechism of the Catholic Church. London: Image Doubleday, 1995.

Clayton, Philip and Arthur Peacocke (eds), *In Whom We Live and Move and Have Our Being: Panentheistic Reflections on God's Presence in a Scientific World*. Grand Rapids, MI: Eerdmans, 2004.

Congar, Yves, *I Believe in the Holy Spirit*. New York: Crossroad, 2000.

Dreyer, Elizabeth A., *Holy Power, Holy Presence: Rediscovering Medieval Metaphors for the Holy Spirit*. New York: Paulist Press, 2007.

Dunn, James D. G., *Baptism in the Holy Spirit: A Re-examination of the New Testament Teaching on the Gift of the Spirit in Relation to Pentecostalism Today*. Philadelphia, PA: Westminster Press, 1970.

—, *The Christ and the Spirit*, vol. 2. Grand Rapids, MI: Eerdmans, 1998.

Fee, Gordon D., *Gospel and Spirit: Issues in New Testament Hermeneutics*. Peabody, MA: Hendrickson, 1991.

—, *God's Empowering Presence: The Holy Spirit in the Letters of Paul*. Peabody, MA: Hendrickson Publishers, 1994.

Fowl, Stephen E., *Engaging Scripture: A Model for Theological Interpretation*. Eugene, OR: Wipf and Stock, 2008.

Gavrilyuk, Paul L. and Sarah Coakley (eds), *The Spiritual Senses: Perceiving God in Western Christianity*. Cambridge: Cambridge University Press, 2012.

Goff, Jr., James R., *Fields White Unto Harvest: Charles F. Parham and the Missionary Origins of Pentecostalism*. Fayetteville: University of Arkansas Press, 1988.

González, Justo L., *A History of Christian Thought*, vol. 1, revised edition. Nashville, TN: Abingdon Press, 1987.

Gunkel, Hermann, *The Influence of the Holy Spirit: The Popular View of the Apostolic Age and the Teachings of the Apostle Paul*, trans. Roy, A. Harrisville and Philip A. Quanbeck II. Philadelphia, PA: Fortress Press, 1979.

Gunter, Stephen W. and Scott J. Jones et. al., *Wesley and the Quadrilateral*. Nashville, TN: Abingdon Press, 1997.

Gunton, Colin E. (ed.), *The Cambridge Companion to Christian Doctrine*. Cambridge: Cambridge University Press, 1997.

Hanson, R. P. C., *The Search for the Christian Doctrine of God: The Arian Controversy, 318–381*. Grand Rapids, MI: Baker Academic, 2005.

Holmes, Michael W., *The Apostolic Fathers in English*, 3rd edition. Grand Rapids, MI: Baker Academic, 2006.

Hunter, Cornelius G., *Science's Blind Spot: The Unseen Religion of Scientific Naturalism*. Grand Rapids, MI: Brazos Press, 2007.

Irenaeus of Lyons, *On the Apostolic Preaching*, trans. John Behr. Crestwood, NY: St. Vladimir's Seminary Press, 1997.

Jenson, Robert W., "You Wonder Where the Spirit Went," *Pro Ecclesia* 2 (1993): 296–304.

Kinnamon, Michael (ed.), *Signs of the Spirit: Official Report of the Seventh Assembly of the World Council of Churches*. Grand Rapids, MI: Eerdmans, 1991.

Knight III, Henry H., *The Presence of God in the Christian Life: John Wesley and the Means of Grace*. Metuchen, NJ: Scarecrow Press, 1992.

Kuhn, Thomas S., *The Structure of Scientific Revolutions*, 3rd edition. Chicago: University of Chicago Press, 1996.

Lederle, H. I., *Treasures Old and New: Interpretation of "Spirit-Baptism" in the Charismatic Renewal Movement*. Peabody, MA: Hendrickson, 1988.

Levering, Matthew, "The Holy Spirit in the Trinitarian Communion: 'Love' and 'Gift'?" *International Journal of Systematic Theology* 16.2 (2014): 126–42.

Levison, John R., "Did the Spirit Withdraw from Israel?" *New Testament Studies* 43 (1997): 35–57.

—, *Filled with the Spirit*. Grand Rapids, MI: Eerdmans, 2009.

—, *Inspired: The Holy Spirit and the Mind of Faith*. Grand Rapids, MI: Eerdmans, 2013.

Lim, Bo H. and Daniel Castelo, *Hosea*, Two Horizons Old Testament Commentary Series. Grand Rapids, MI: Eerdmans, forthcoming.

Lossky, Vladimir, *In the Image and Likeness of God*. Crestwood, NY: St. Vladimir's Seminary Press, 2001.

Macchia, Frank D., *Baptized in the Spirit: A Global Pentecostal Theology*. Grand Rapids, MI: Zondervan, 2006.

McDonnell, Kilian and George T. Montague, *Christian Initiation and Baptism in the Holy Spirit*, 2nd revised edition. Collegeville, PA: Liturgical Press, 1994.

Menzies, Robert P., *Empowered for Witness: The Spirit in Luke-Acts*. Sheffield: Sheffield Academic Press, 1994.

Miller, Donald E. and Tetsunao Yamamori, *Global Pentecostalism: The New Face of Christian Social Engagement*. Berkeley: University of California, 2007.

Montague, George T., *The Holy Spirit: The Growth of a Biblical Tradition*. Eugene, OR: Wipf and Stock Publishers, 2006.

Newbigin, Lesslie, *The Household of God: Lectures on the Nature of the Church*. New York: Friendship Press, 1954.

Pannenberg, Wolfhart, Avery Dulles, S. J. and Carl E. Braaten (eds), *Spirit, Faith, and Church*. Philadelphia, PA: Westminster Press, 1970.

Papanikolaou, Aristotle and George E. Demacopoulos (eds), *Orthodox Readings of Augustine*. Crestwood, NY: St. Vladimir's Seminary Press, 2008.

Pinnock, Clark H., *Flame of Love: A Theology of the Holy Spirit*. Downers Grove, IL: InterVarsity, 1996.

Radde-Gallwitz, Andrew, *Basil of Caesarea: A Guide to His Life and Doctrine*. Eugene, OR: Cascade, 2012.

Rogers, Jr., Eugene F., *After the Spirit: A Constructive Pneumatology from Resources Outside the Modern West*. Grand Rapids, MI: Eerdmans, 2005.

Smith, James K. A., *Speech and Theology: Language and the Logic of Incarnation*. London: Routledge, 2002.

—, *Introducing Radical Orthodoxy: Mapping a Post-Secular Theology*. Grand Rapids, MI: Baker Academic, 2004.

—, "The Spirit, Religions, and the World as Sacrament: A Response to Amos Yong's Pneumatological Assist," *Journal of Pentecostal Theology* 15.2 (2007): 251–61.

—, *Thinking in Tongues: Pentecostal Contributions to Christian Philosophy*. Grand Rapids, MI: Eerdmans, 2010.

Smith, James K. A. and Amos Yong (eds), *Science and the Spirit: A Pentecostal Engagement with the Sciences*. Bloomington: Indiana University Press, 2010.

Stott, John R. W., *Baptism and Fullness: The Work of the Holy Spirit Today*. Downers Grove, IL: InterVarsity, 1979.

Stronstad, Roger, *The Charismatic Theology of St. Luke*. Peabody, MA: Hendrickson Publishers, 1984.

Sullivan, Francis A., *Charism and Charismatic Renewal*. Ann Arbor, MI: Servant Books, 1982.

Synan, Vinson (ed.), *Aspects of Pentecostal-Charismatic Origins*. Plainfield, NJ: Logos International, 1975.

Thiselton, Anthony C., *The Holy Spirit—In Biblical Teaching, through the Centuries, and Today*. Grand Rapids, MI: Eerdmans, 2013.

Thorsen, Donald, *The Wesleyan Quadrilateral*. Grand Rapids, MI: Zondervan, 1990.

Vanhoozer, Kevin J., *The Drama of Doctrine: A Canonical-Linguistic Approach to Christian Theology*. Louisville, KY: Westminster John Knox, 2005.

Volf, Miroslav and Michael Welker (eds), *God's Life in Trinity*. Minneapolis: Fortress Press, 2006.

Wall, Robert W. with Richard B. Steele, *1 & 2 Timothy and Titus*. Grand Rapids, MI: Eerdmans, 2012.

Ware, Kallistos, *The Orthodox Way*, revised edition. Crestwood, NY: St. Vladimir's Seminary Press, 1979.

Webster, John, *Holiness*. Grand Rapids, MI: Eerdmans, 2003.

—, *Holy Scripture: A Dogmatic Sketch*. Cambridge: Cambridge University Press, 2003.

—, *The Domain of the Word: Scripture and Theological Reason*. London: T & T Clark, 2012.

Webster, John, Kathryn Tanner and Iain Torrance (eds), *The Oxford Handbook of Systematic Theology*. Oxford: Oxford University Press, 2007.

Weinandy, Thomas, *The Father's Spirit of Sonship: Reconceiving the Trinity*. Eugene, OR: Wipf and Stock, 2010.

Welker, Michael, *God the Spirit*. Minneapolis: Fortress, 1994.

Welker, Michael (ed.), *The Work of the Spirit: Pneumatology and Pentecostalism*. Grand Rapids, MI: Eerdmans, 2006.

Wells, Samuel, *Improvisation: The Drama of Christian Ethics*. Grand Rapids, MI: Brazos Press, 2004.

Westphal, Merold, *Suspicion and Faith: The Religious Uses of Modern Atheism*. New York: Fordham University Press, 1998.

Wilken, Robert Louis, *The Spirit of Early Christian Thought: Seeking the Face of God*. New Haven, CT: Yale University Press, 2003.

Williams, Rowan, *The Wound of Knowledge: Christian Spirituality from the New Testament to Saint John of the Cross*. Lanham, MD: Cowley, 1990.

Winn, Christian T. Collins (ed.), *From the Margins: A Celebration of the Theological Work of Donald W. Dayton*. Eugene, OR: Pickwick, 2007.

Wright, N. T., *The New Testament and the People of God*. Minneapolis: Fortress Press, 1992.

Yong, Amos, *Discerning the Spirits: A Pentecostal-Charismatic Contribution to Christian Theology of Religions*. Sheffield: Sheffield Academic Press, 2000.

—, *Spirit-Word-Community: Theological Hermeneutics in Trinitarian Perspective*. Eugene, OR: Wipf and Stock, 2002.

—, *Beyond the Impasse: Toward a Pneumatological Theology of Religions*. Grand Rapids, MI: Baker Academic, 2003.

—, *The Spirit Poured Out on All Flesh: Pentecostalism and the Possibility of Global Theology*. Grand Rapids, MI: Baker Academic, 2005.

INDEX

CPSIA information can be obtained
at www.ICGtesting.com
Printed in the USA
LVOW10s1952291217
561239LV00011B/217/P